Is He Gay?

*For Every Woman Who's Met the Ideal Man
and Is Wondering . . . Why Hasn't He Tried to Kiss Me?*

*Ed Baker & Chris Busick
Illustrated by Ed Baker*

A Fireside Book
Published by Simon & Schuster
New York London Sydney Singapore

Fireside
Rockefeller Center
1230 Avenue of the Americas
New York, NY 10020

Text copyright © 2000 by Ed Baker and Chris Busick
Illustrations copyright © 2000 by Ed Baker
FIRESIDE and colophon are registered trademarks of Simon & Schuster, Inc.

Designed by Gabriel Levine

Manufactured in the United States of America

10   9   8   7   6   5   4   3   2   1

Library of Congress Cataloging-in-Publication Data is available.

ISBN 0-684-86793-1

Special thanks to:

Our families for their unconditional love, support, and confidence. We love you!
Our friends for input, advice, favors, and fun.
Two women who know how to party, Simon & Schuster's Airié
Dekidjiev and ICM's Karen Gerwin. Also, Gheña and Greg.

Special <u>no</u> thanks to:

All proponents of hatred, bigotry, and/or discrimination.

Dedicated to all the women who've ended up "just friends."

...well is he?

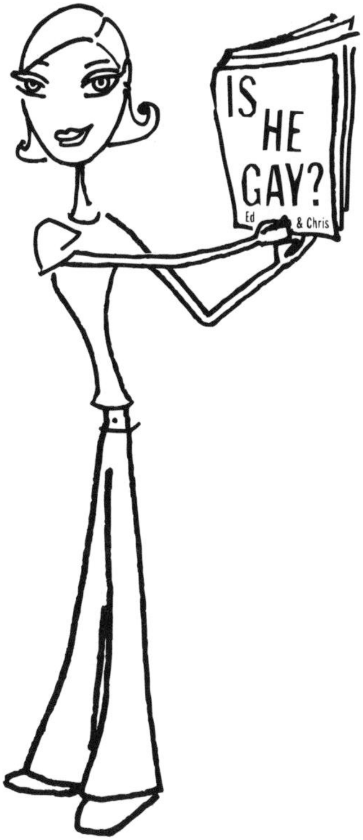
IS
HE
GAY?
Ed
& Chris

You've finally met a guy who makes every moment feel like a Kodak commercial. Your inner voice cries, "I DO!" but your sex drive screams, "WE DON'T!" As your relationship reaches new heights of intimacy, the snapshots seem clearly platonic. You ask yourself, "Why didn't I see this coming?" We answer, "Because you haven't read this book."

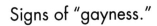

LEGEND *

Signs of "gayness."

DUH.

Girl's thought process.

Endnotes.

*What the symbols mean.

ONCE UPON A TIME

. . . there was a fabulous young woman (just like you!) . . . who was about to meet the perfect man in the most unlikely of places . . .

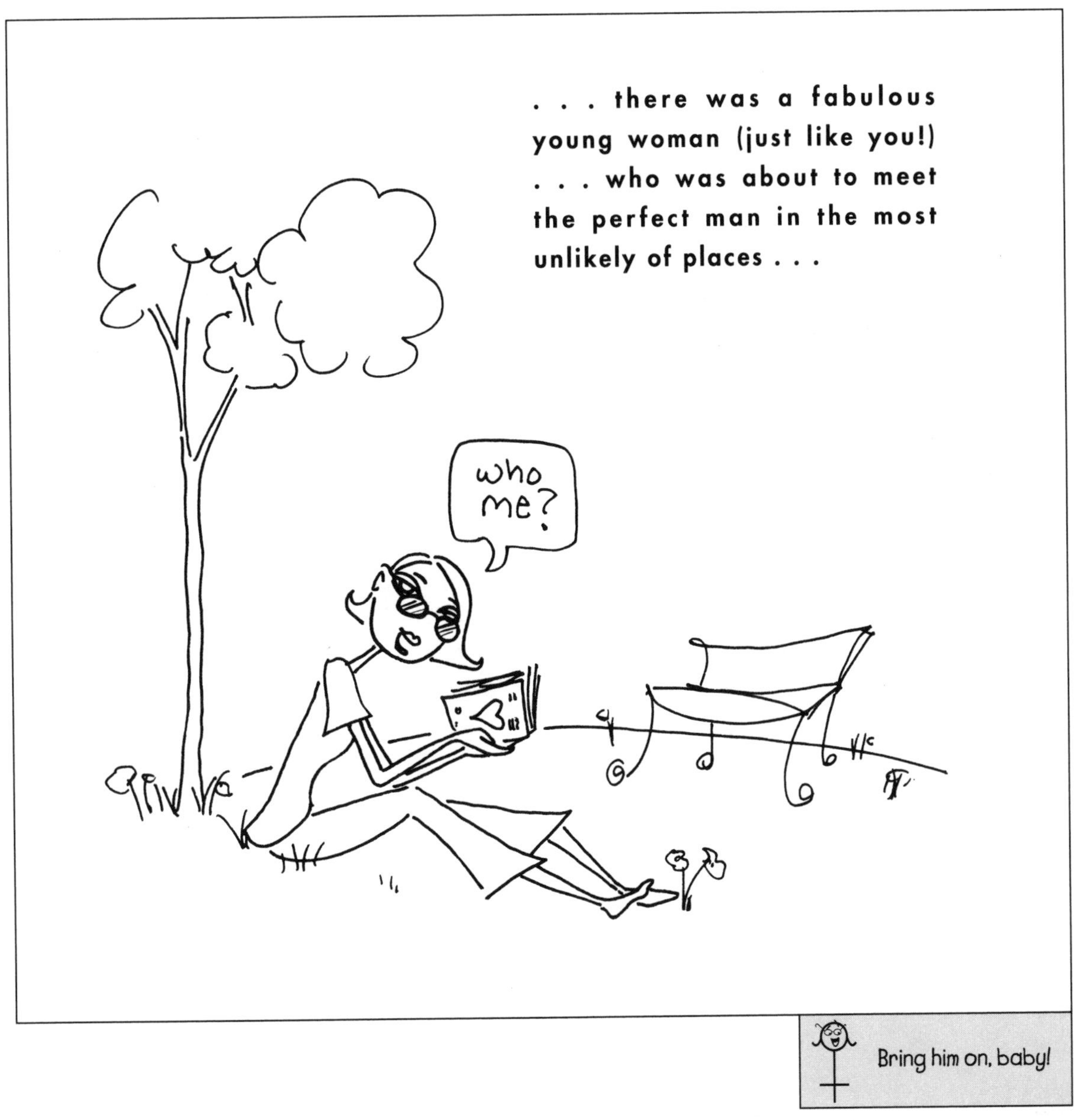
who me?

Bring him on, baby!

AT BARNEYS*

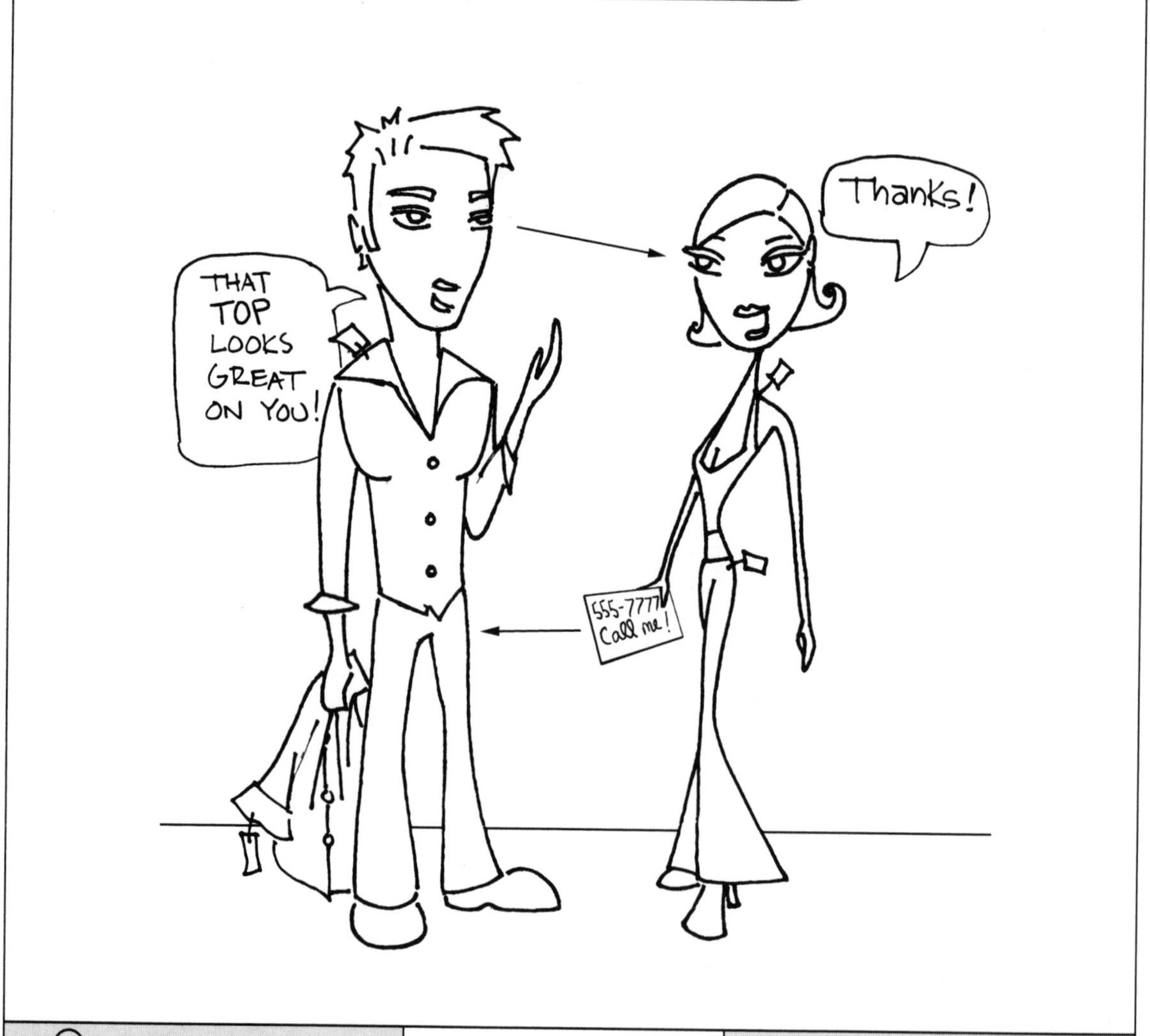
THAT TOP LOOKS GREAT ON YOU!
Thanks!
555-7777 Call me!

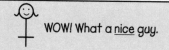

WOW! What a <u>nice</u> guy.

*An American institution of fashion.

. . . he's too pretty . . .

. . . designer clothing (tucked/tight) . . .

. . . he looks in your eyes, <u>not</u> at your boobs . . .

. . . you gave him YOUR number . . .*

*He didn't ask for it.

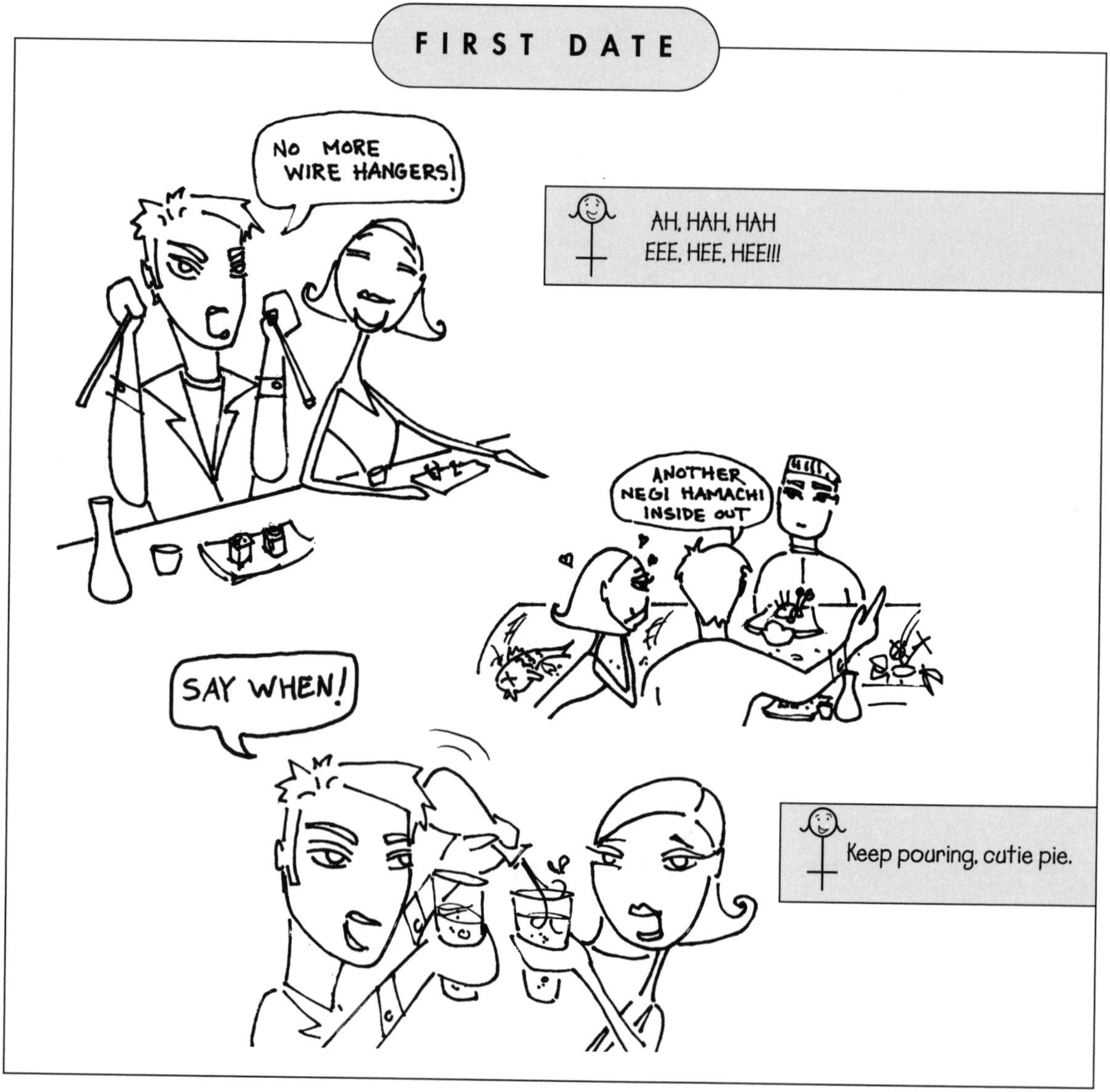
FIRST DATE
NO MORE WIRE HANGERS!
AH, HAH, HAH
EEE, HEE, HEE!!!
ANOTHER NEGI HAMACHI INSIDE OUT
SAY WHEN!
Keep pouring, cutie pie.

. . . you go dutch . . .

. . . he's not getting you drunk, <u>you</u> are . . .

. . . comments on your nail polish & asks if it's "MAC . . ."

. . . sushi . . .

. . . fabulous sense of humor . . .

TRAGIC DIVAS*

*Joan Crawford, Bette Davis, Eartha Kitt, Mae West, Judy & Liza, George Michael, Doris Day, Harvey Fierstein, Ethel Merman, Eva Perón, Streisand, & Cher.

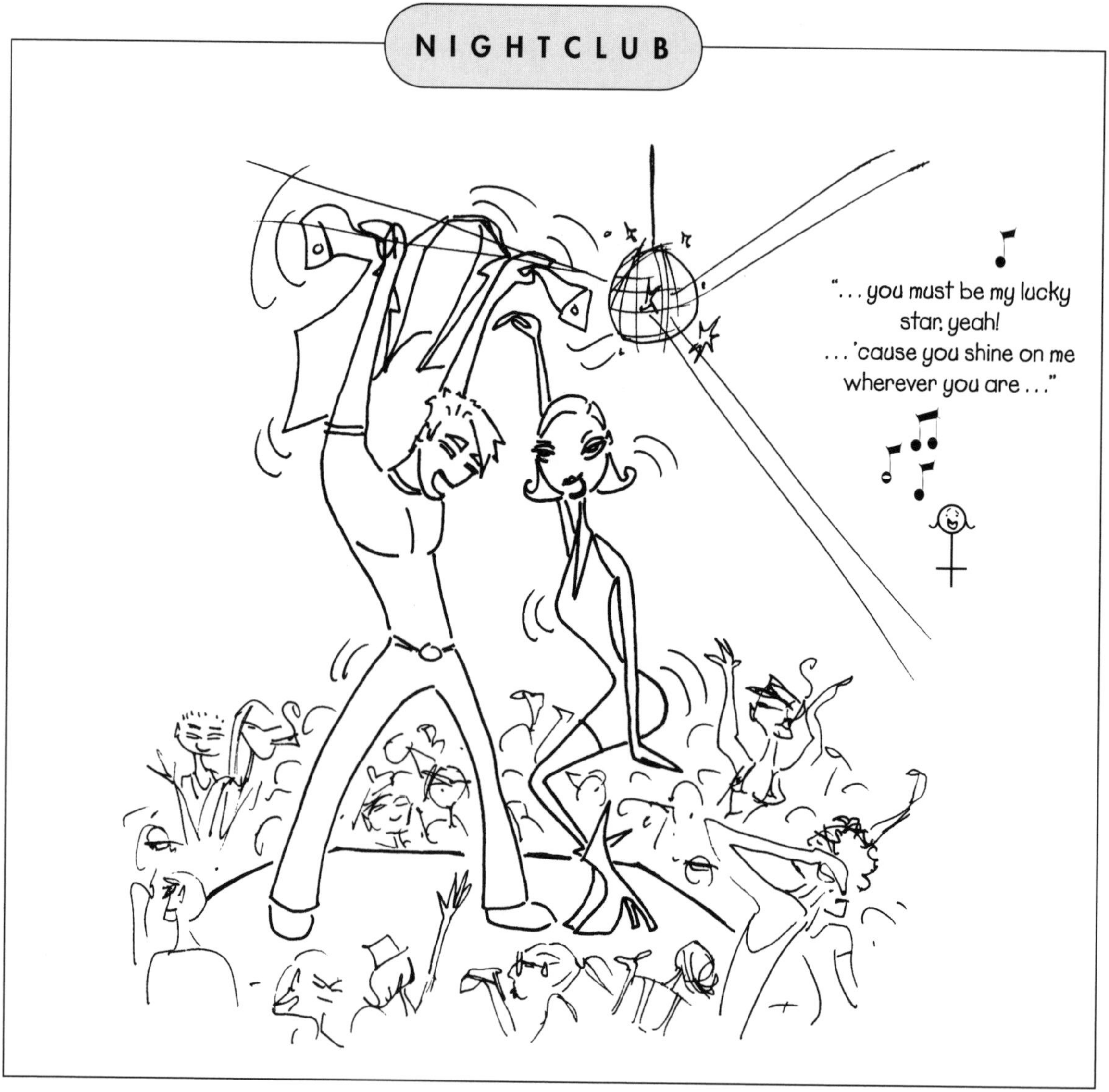
NIGHTCLUB
"... you must be my lucky star, yeah!
...'cause you shine on me wherever you are..."

. . . awesome dancer . . .

. . . performs unusual moves: air sways, hip rolls, high kicks . . .*

. . . gets easily excited . . .

. . . dances shirtless . . .

. . . screams when they play "Techno Celine" . . .

MADONNA

*A type of gay gymnastic or expression of sheer excitement/freedom.

AFTER-HOURS

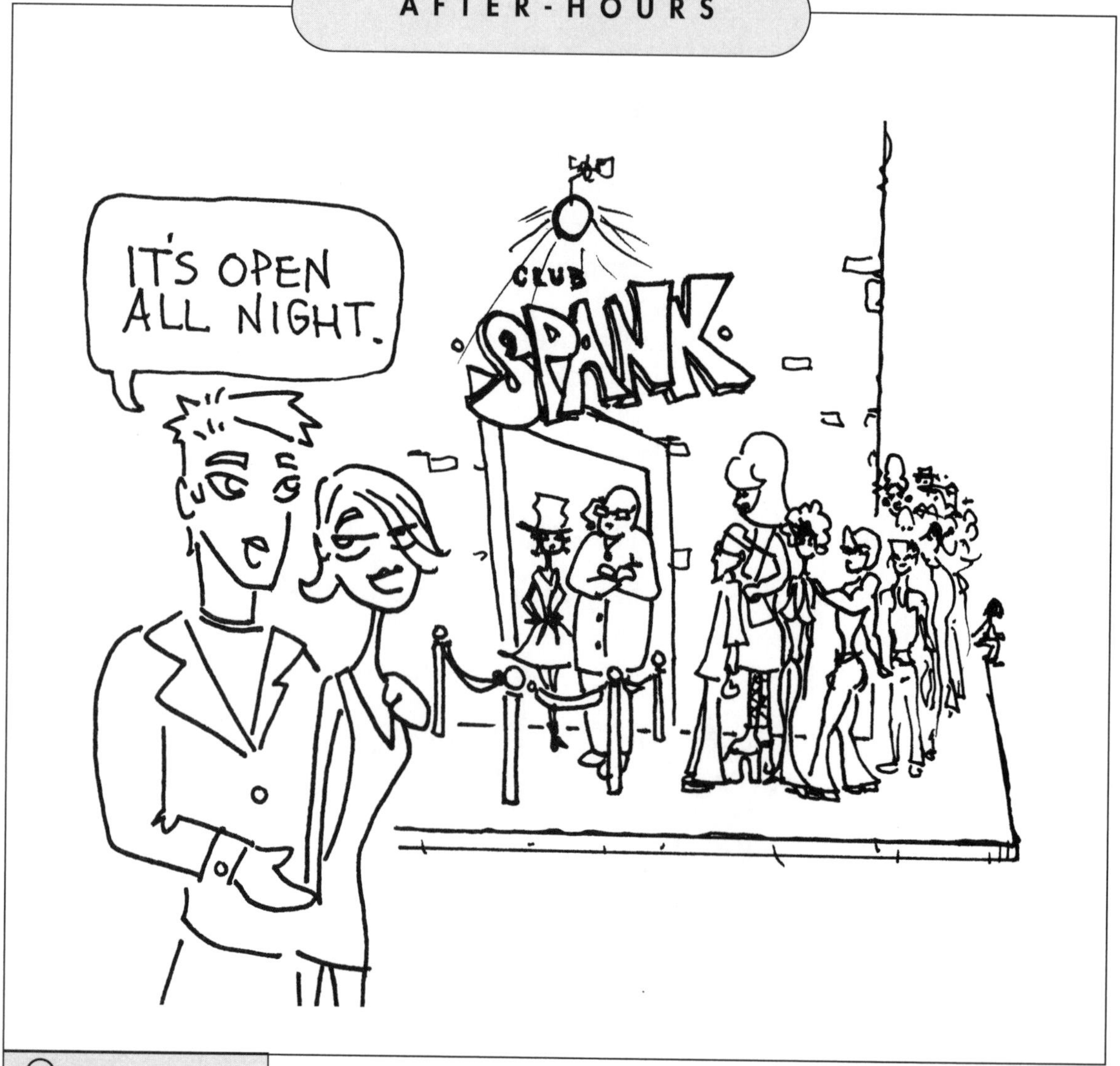
IT'S OPEN ALL NIGHT.
CLUB
SPANK

You are so smart!

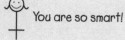

AFTER-HOURS (Backroom)

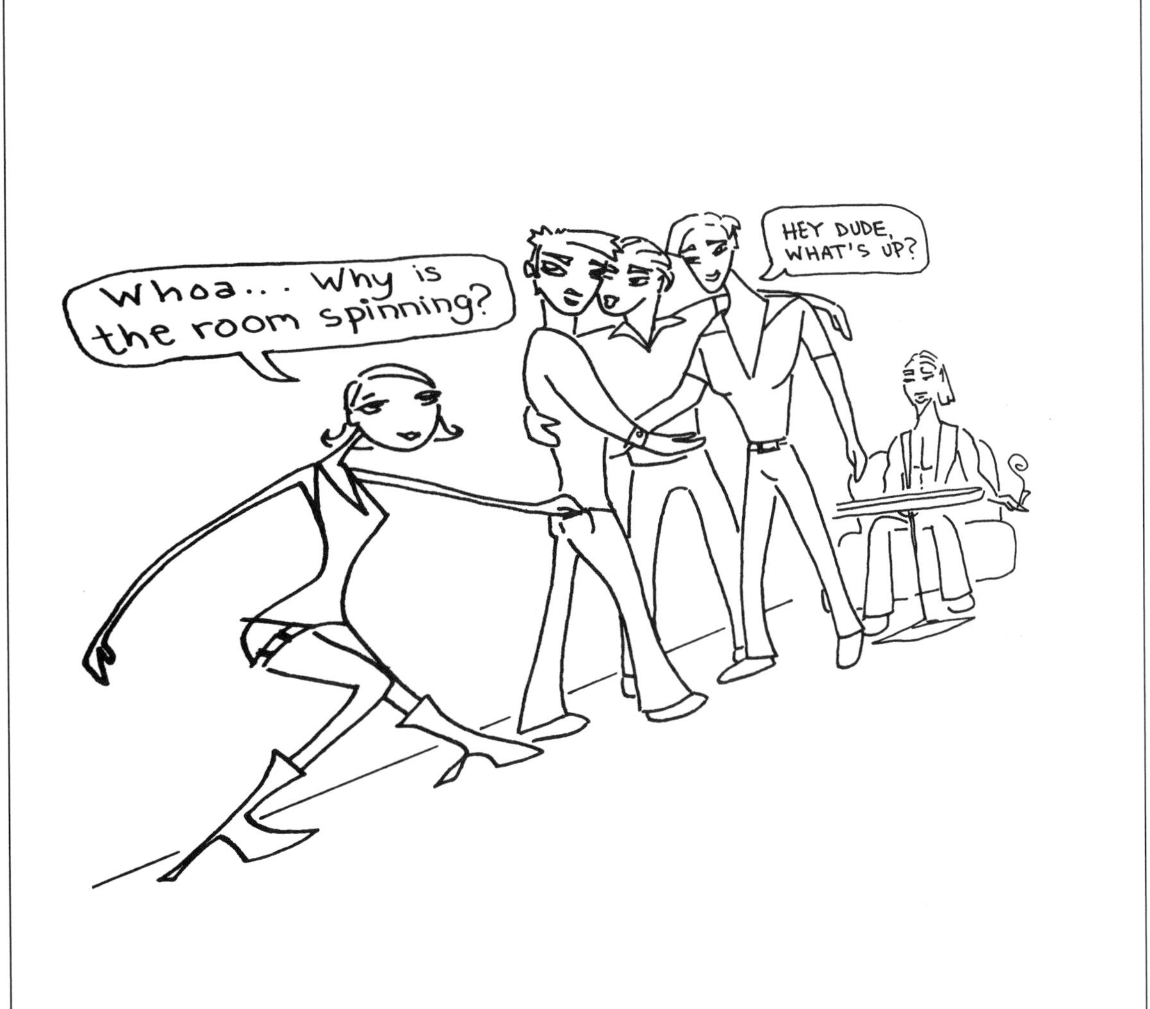
Whoa... Why is the room spinning?
HEY DUDE, WHAT'S UP?

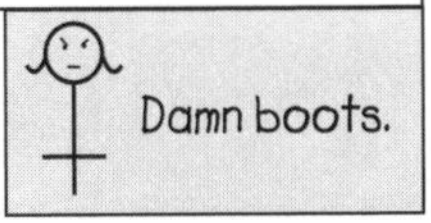
Damn boots.

AFTER-HOURS (Bathroom)

I think, I drank too much.

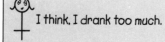

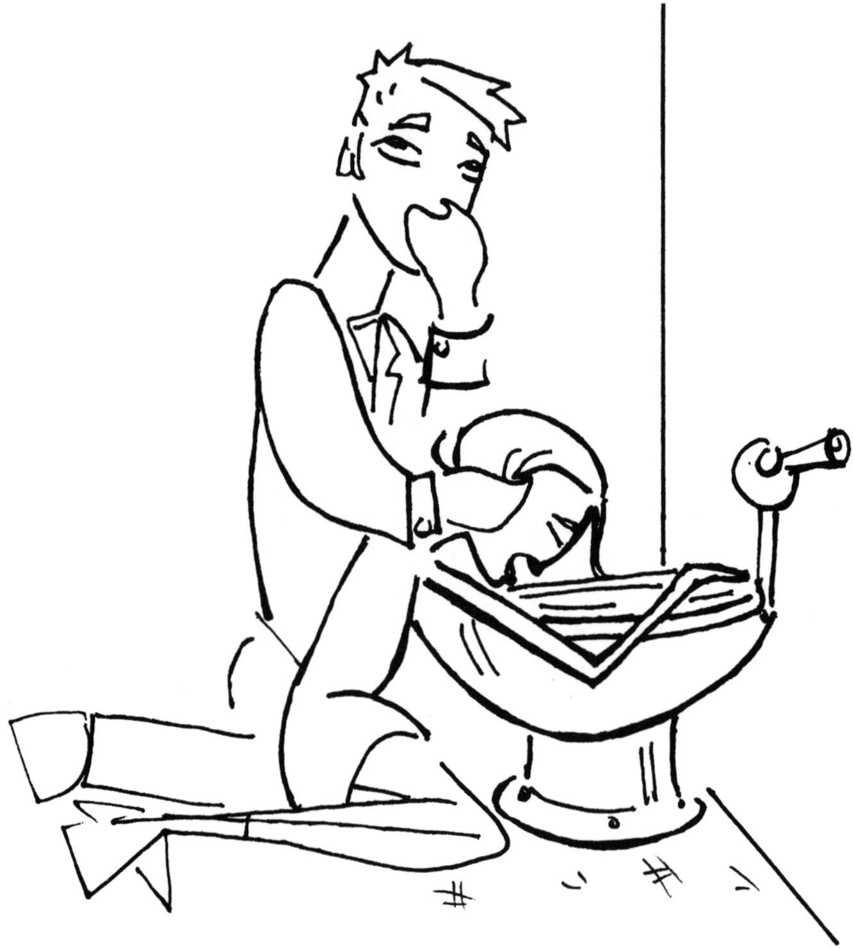

Hints

. . . cute guy friends . . .

. . . warm greetings . . .*

SUPERHINT

HE TAKES CARE OF YOU

*Hugs or kisses both women & men.

SUNRISE

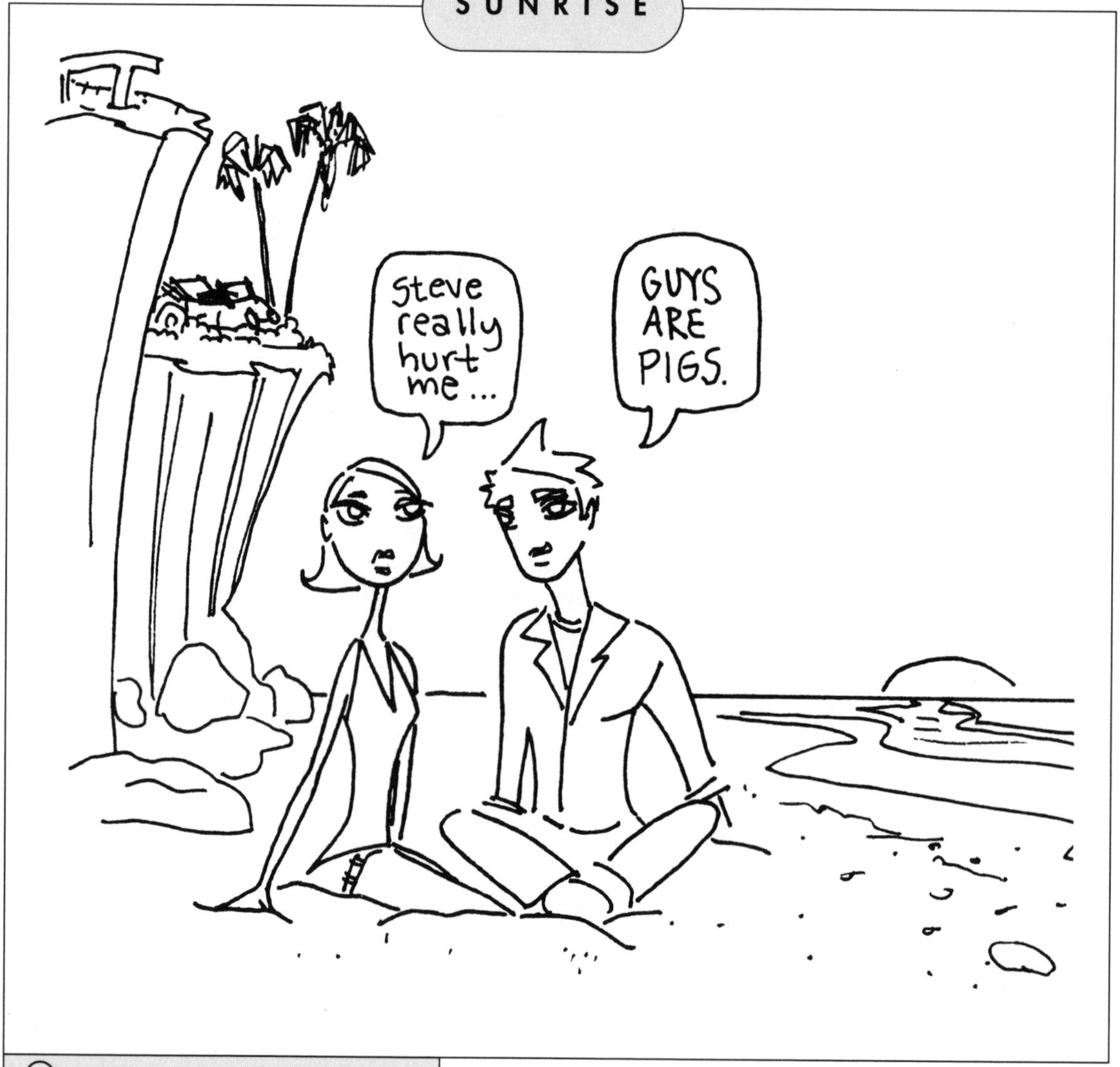
Steve really hurt me...
GUYS ARE PIGS.

It's like he can read my thoughts!!
PLEASE, PLEASE . . . KISS ME!!!

. . . great listener . . .*

. . . wants to know you as a person . . .

. . . no advances . . .

*He really seems to care about your problems & gives you advice
that significantly changes the way you view men.

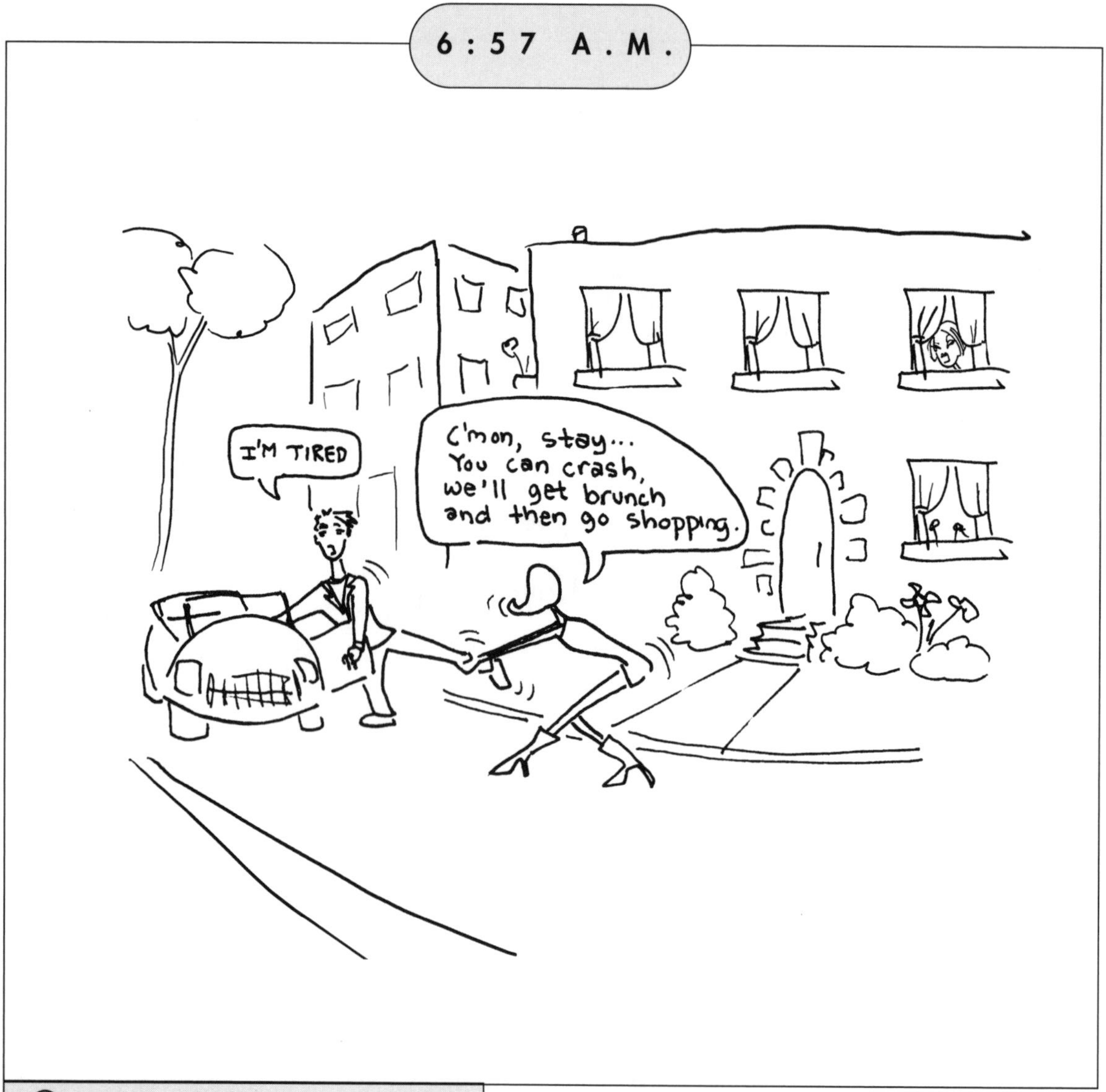
6:57 A.M.
I'M TIRED
C'mon, stay... You can crash, we'll get brunch and then go shopping.

Oooo, playin' hard to get . . . stud muffin!

. . . no kissin' . . .

PLAYS HARD TO GET

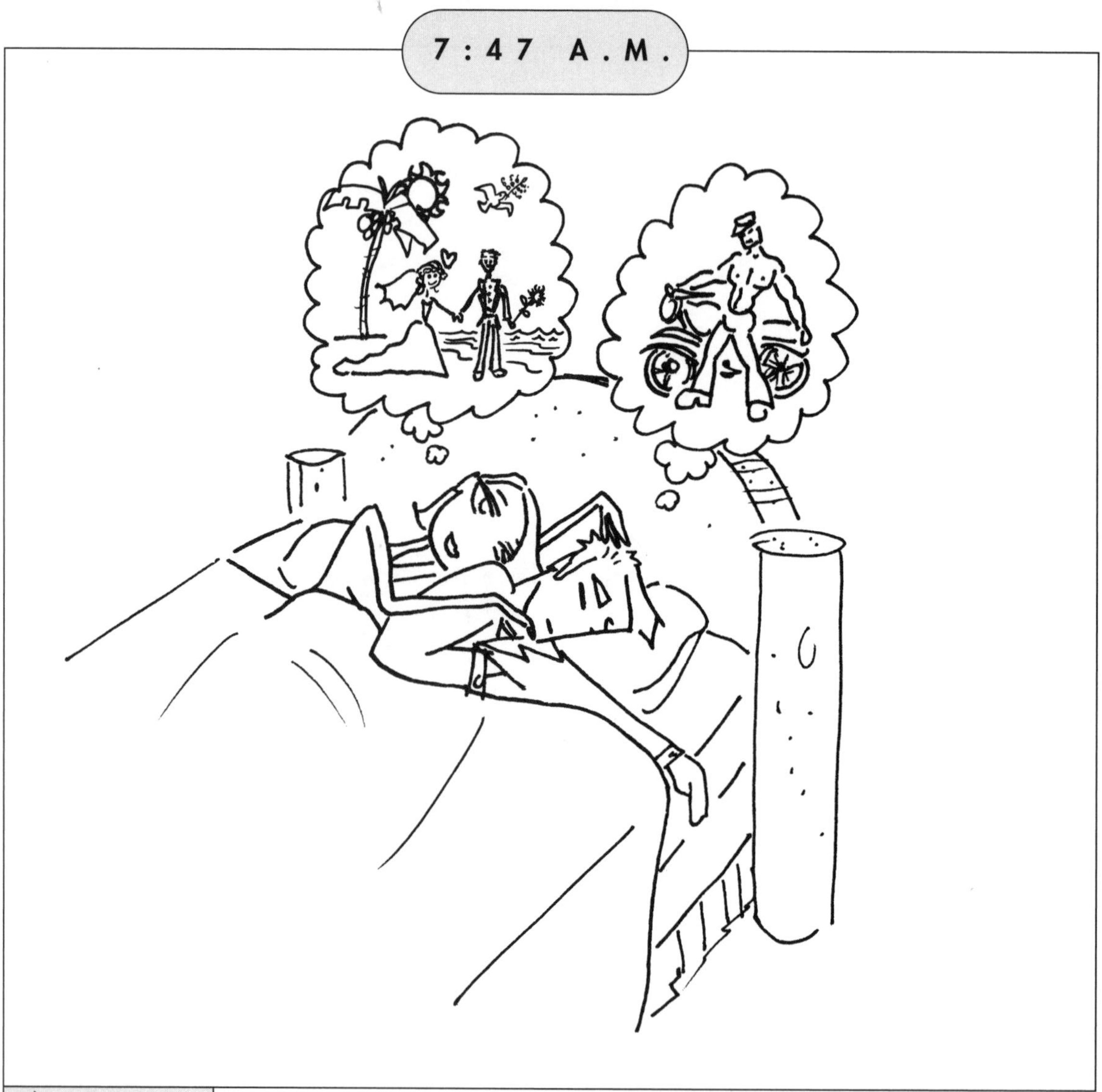
7:47 A.M.

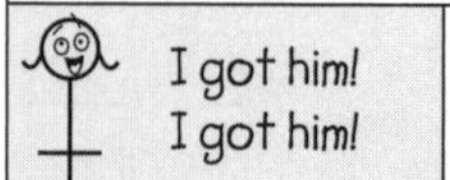
I got him!
I got him!

. . . you spoon him . . .

. . . he goes to sleep . . .*

*Fully clothed.

BRUNCH

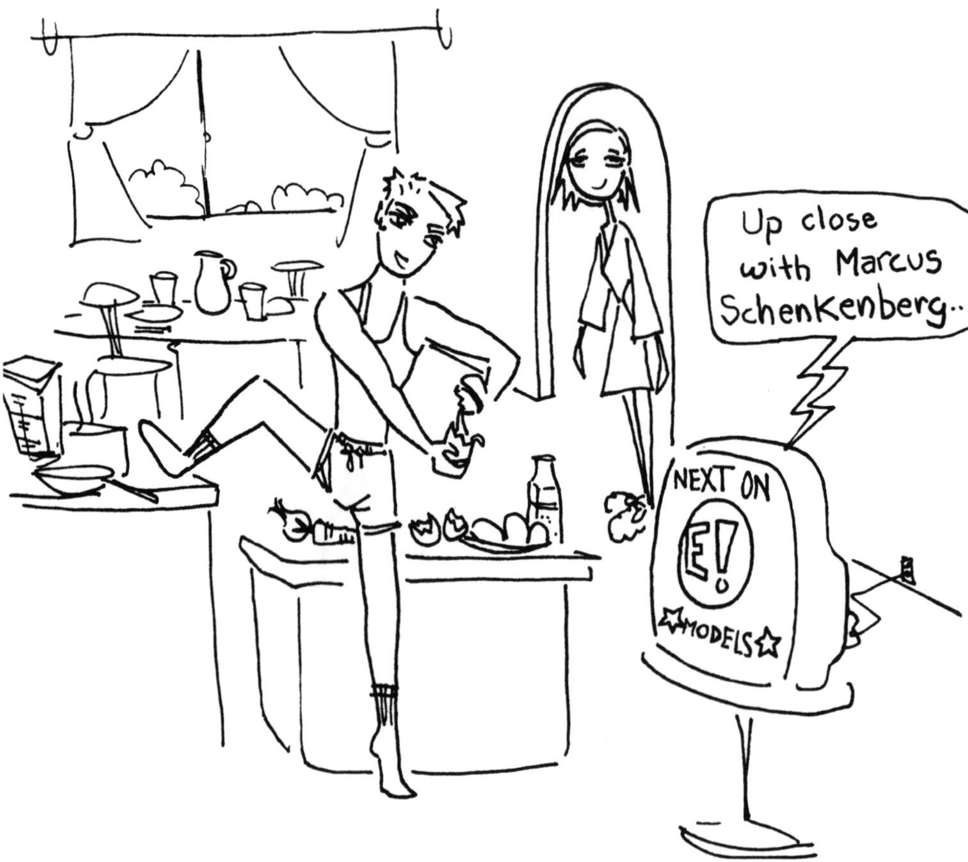

Up close with Marcus Schenkenberg...
NEXT ON
E!
MODELS

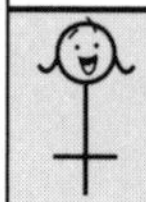
He cooks!

. . . he cooks . . .

. . . egg white omelettes . . .

. . . keeps workout clothes in the car . . .

E!—ENTERTAINMENT TELEVISION

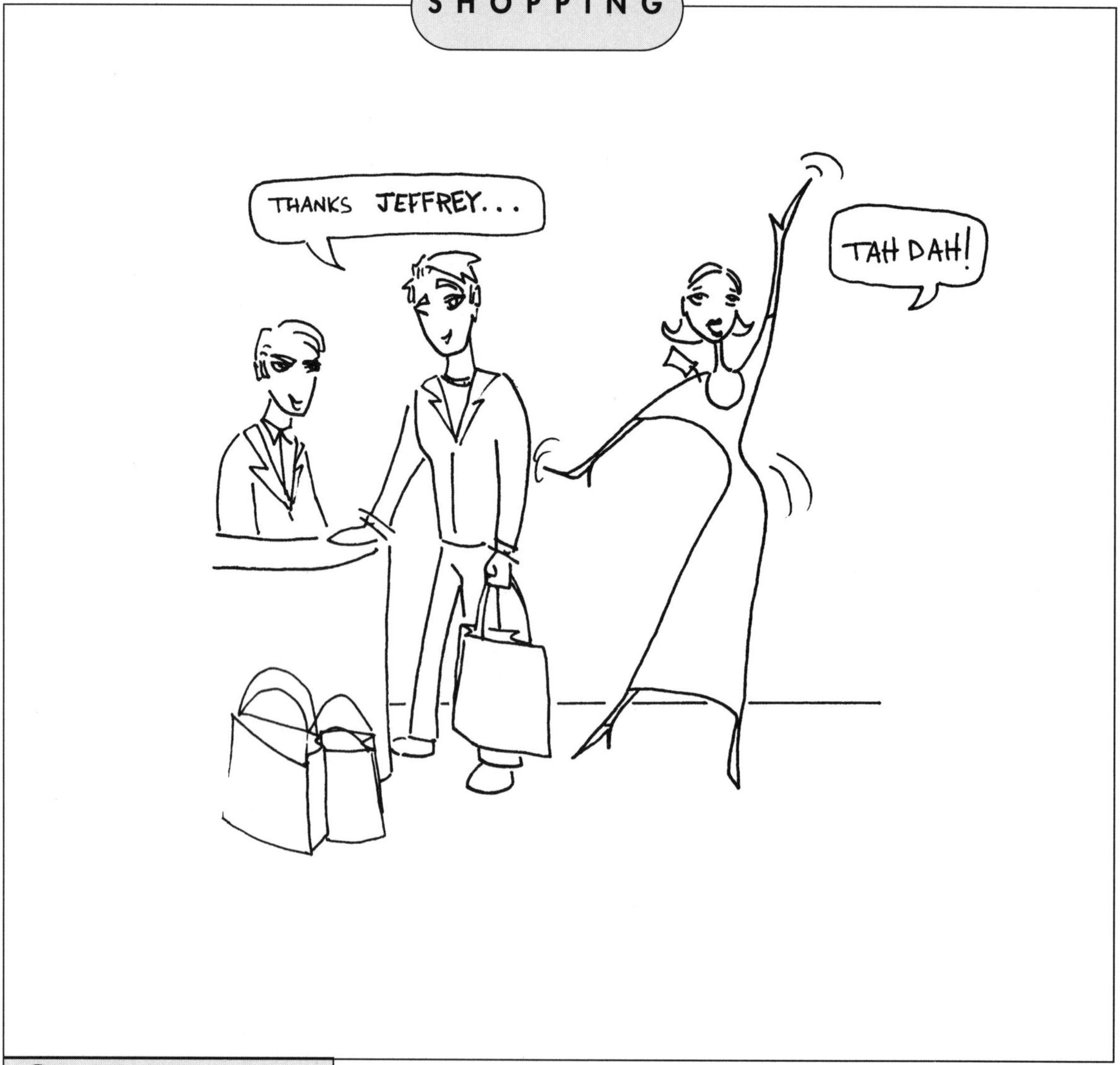
THANKS JEFFREY...
TAH DAH!

Those spinning classes really paid off!

Hints

. . . label whore . . .*

. . . full names . . .**

*Drops designer names . . . e.g., Helmut Lang, Miu-Miu, Prada, Gucci/Tom Ford, Halston, Paul Smith, & La Croix.

**E.g., Jeff=Jeffrey, Chris=Christopher, Mike=Michael, Dave=David, Al=Alexis, Rick=Frederico, Vince=Divine, Abe=Abercrombie, Paul=RuPaul or Pee Wee.

POST-SHOPPING HIGH

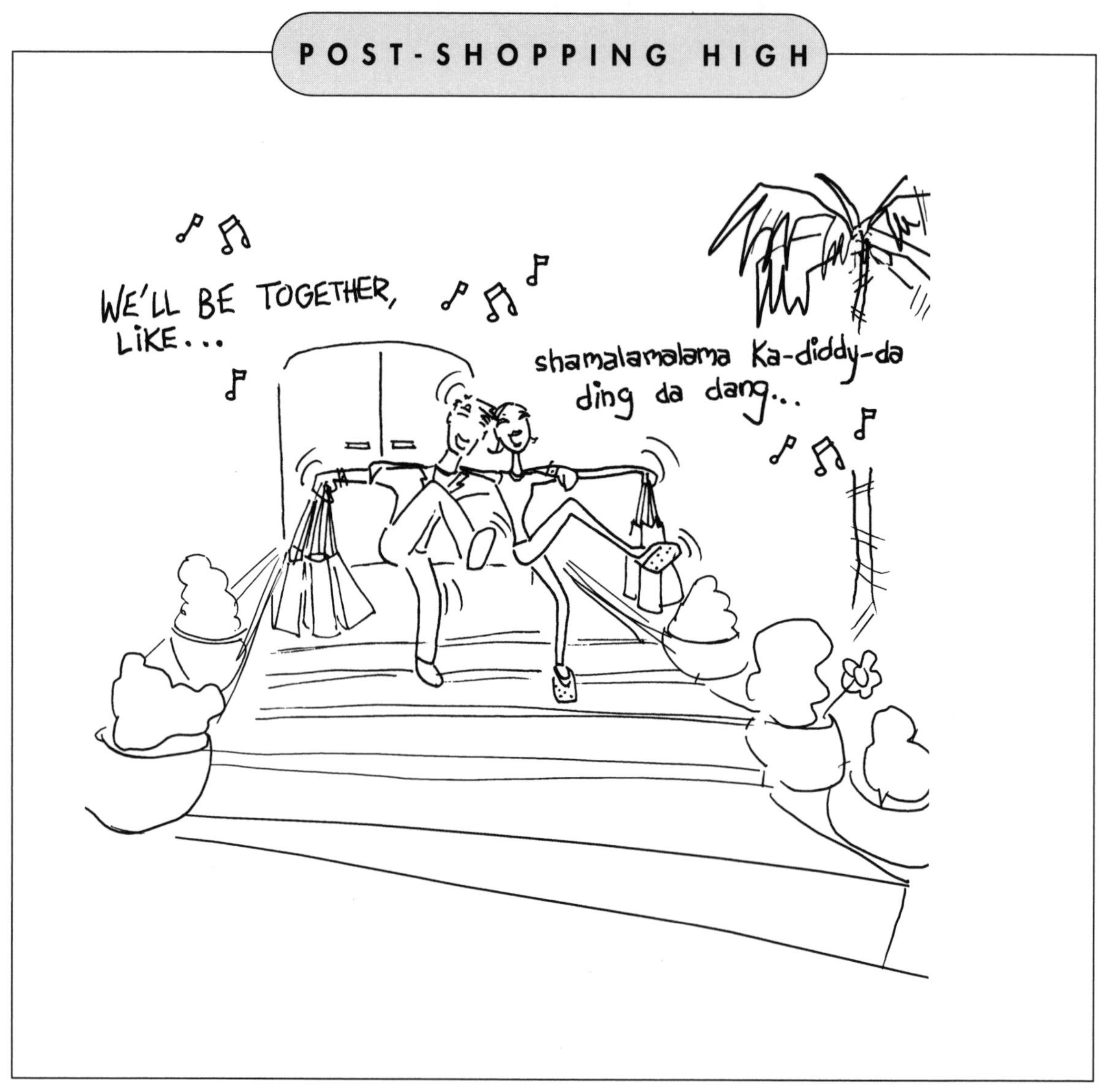
WE'LL BE TOGETHER, LIKE...
shamalamamalama Ka-diddy-da ding da dang...

. . . he can shop till you drop . . .

SHOW TUNES

A LIGHT SNACK

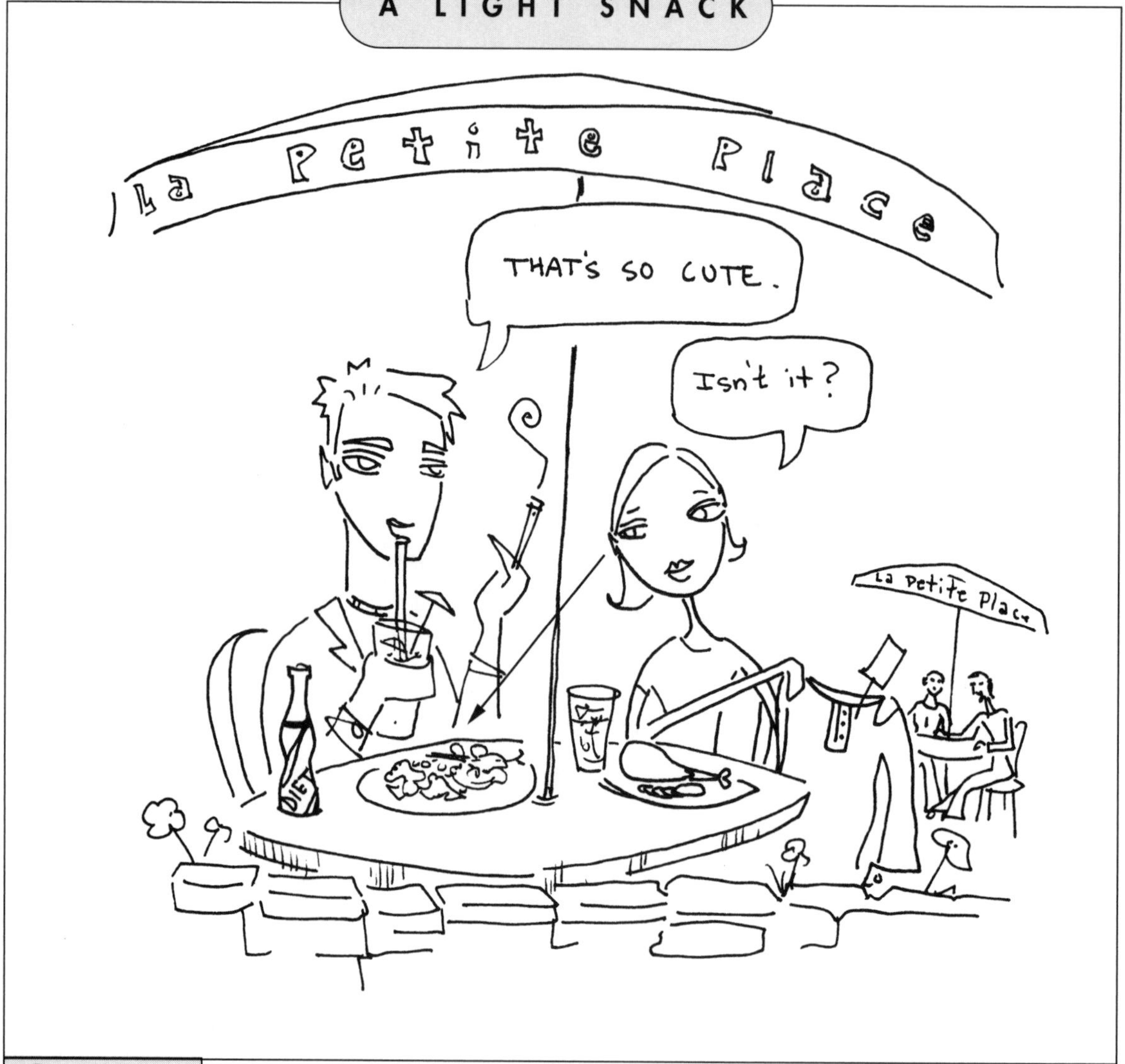

A salad?

Hints

. . . fantastic posture . . .

. . . dramatic body language . . .

. . . suspicious cigarette grip . . .

. . . giggles . . .

SUPERHINT

"CUTE"*

*Also: "Oh . . . No!" "Fantastic," "HOT!" "Super," "Fabulous," "Excuse me?" "Whatever . . . ," "Honey," & "You GO, Girl!"

YOUR FAVORITE STORE!

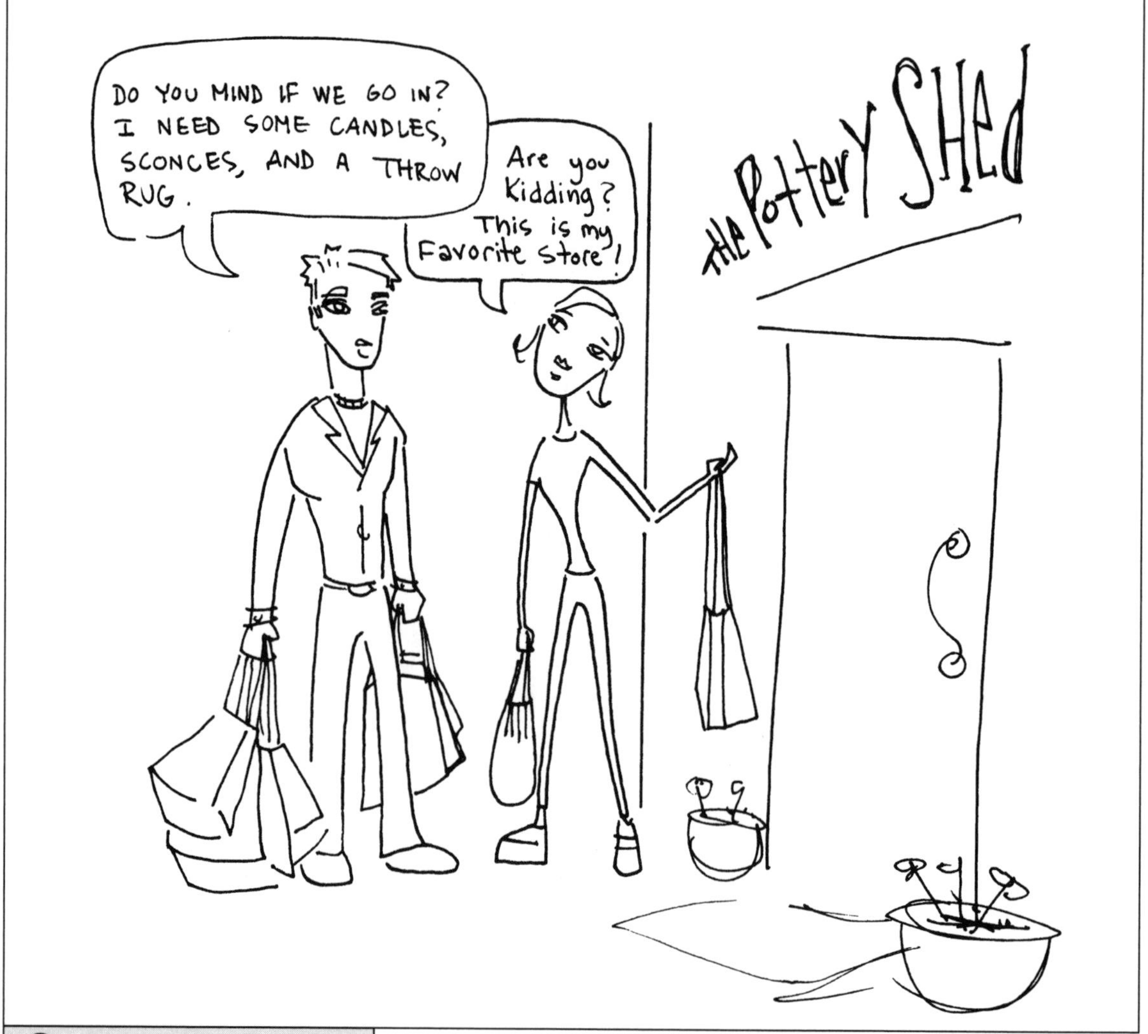
DO YOU MIND IF WE GO IN? I NEED SOME CANDLES, SCONCES, AND A THROW RUG.
Are you kidding? This is my Favorite Store!
the Pottery SHed

We have so much in common!

. . . candles . . .

. . . sconces . . .

. . . throw rug . . .

GOOD-BYE

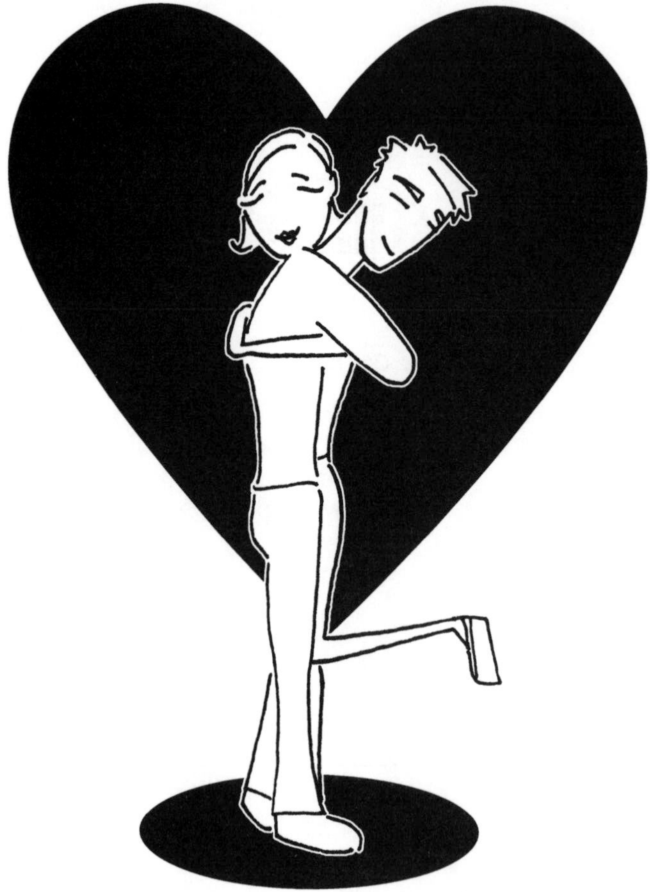

Hints

. . . brotherly hugs . . .

. . . doesn't cop a feel . . .

. . . passionless pecks . . .

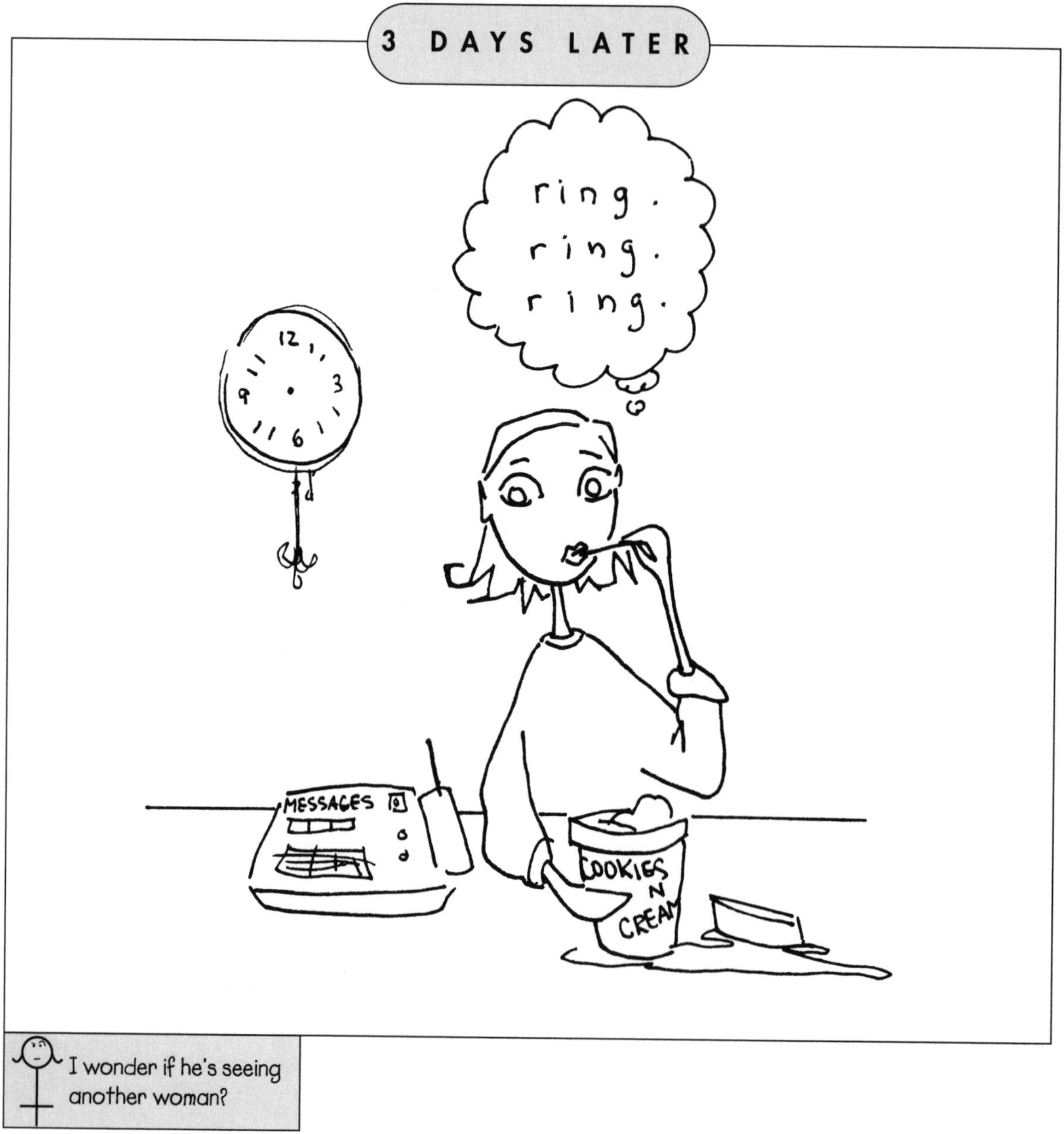
3 DAYS LATER
ring.
ring.
ring.
MESSAGES 0
COOKIES N CREAM
I wonder if he's seeing another woman?

MEANWHILE

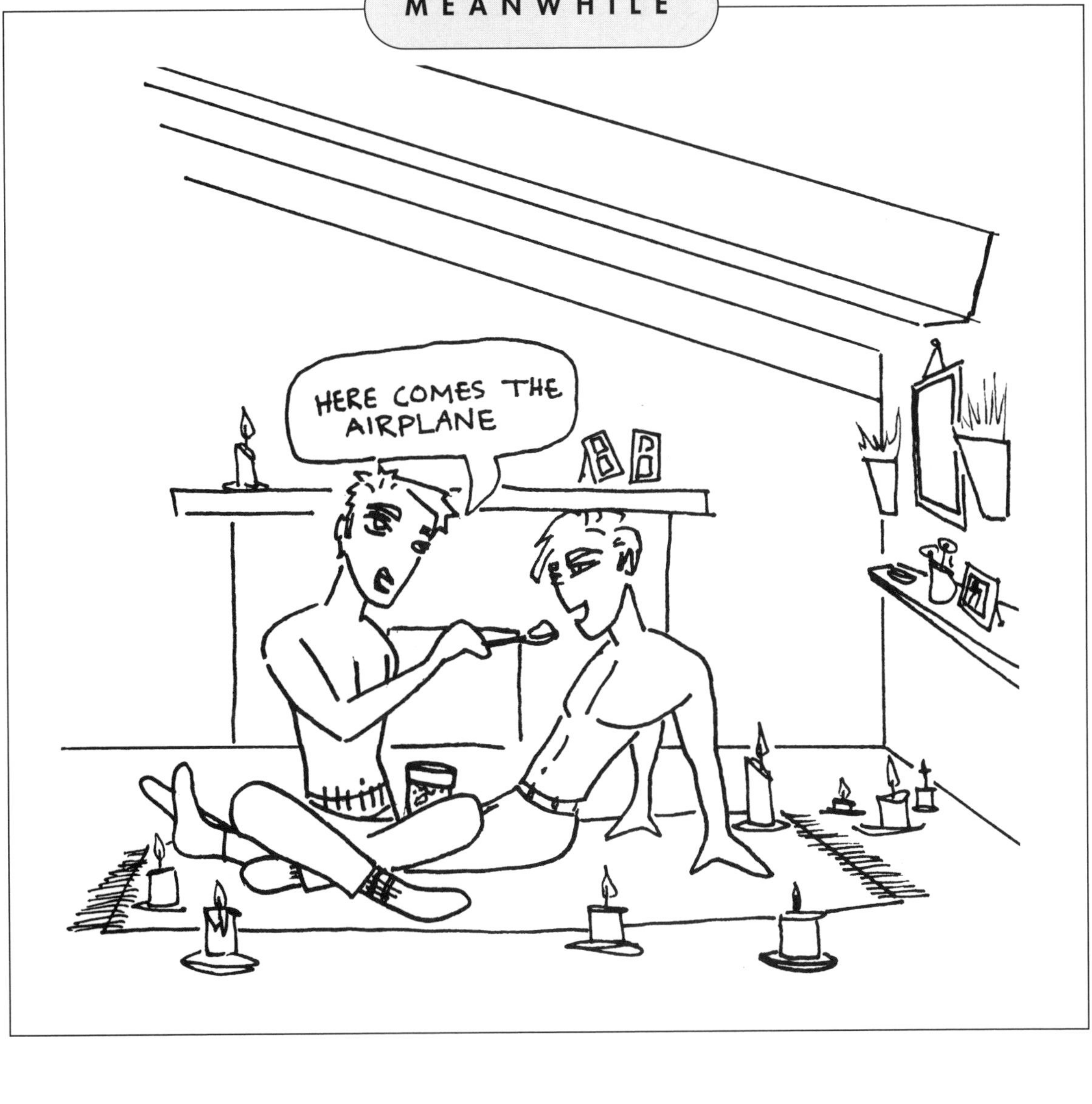
HERE COMES THE AIRPLANE

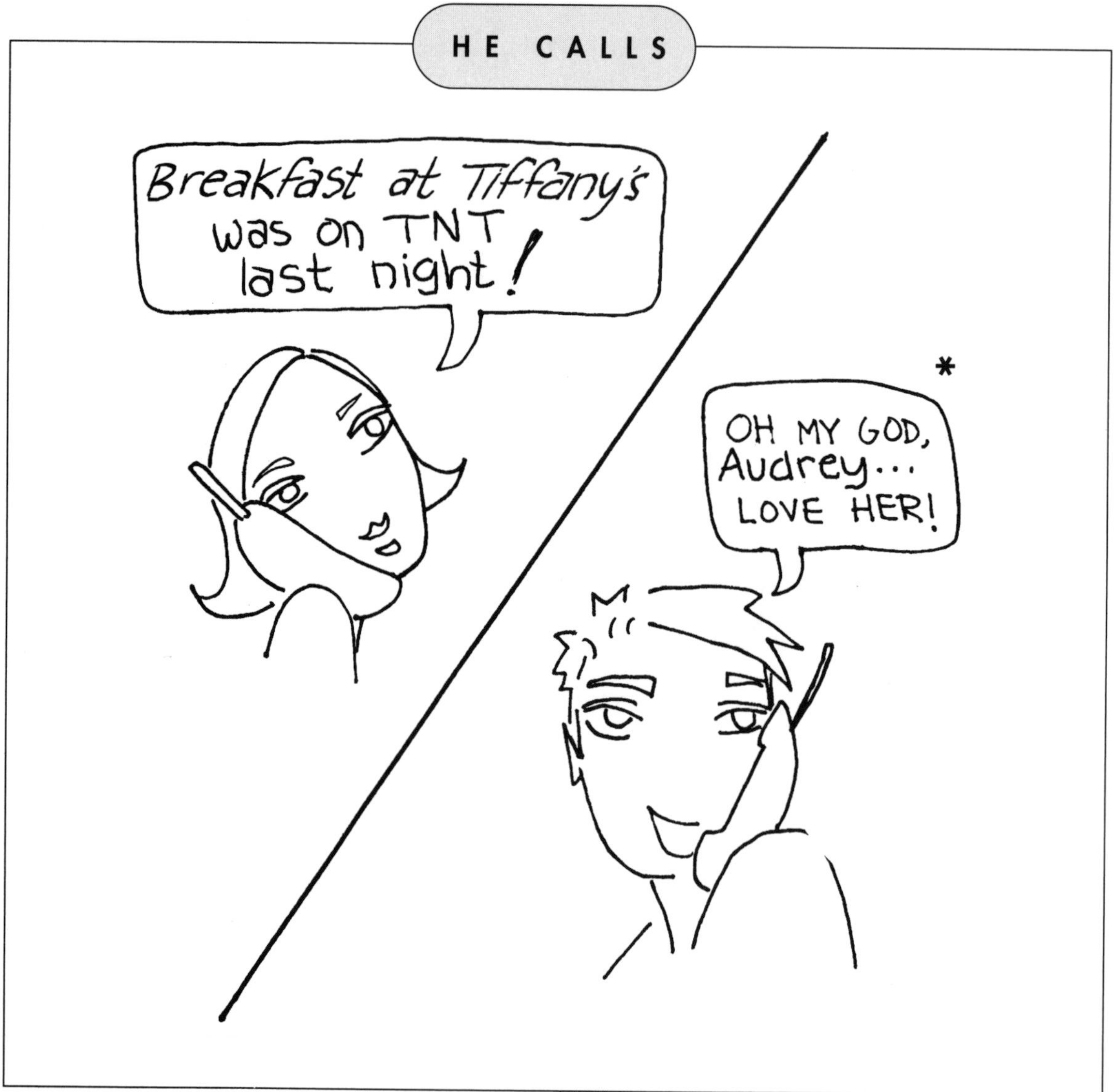
HE CALLS
Breakfast at Tiffany's was on TNT last night!
*
OH MY GOD, Audrey... LOVE HER!

*To gab: **gab** / gab'/ [ME] *colloq n* 1 idle chatter || v **(gabbed; gab-bing)** *vi* 2 to chatter idly.

Hints

. . . idle chatter . . .

SUPERHINT

THEATRICAL INFLECTION*

*"Oh. My. God. <u>LOVE</u> her."

HE CALLS AGAIN!

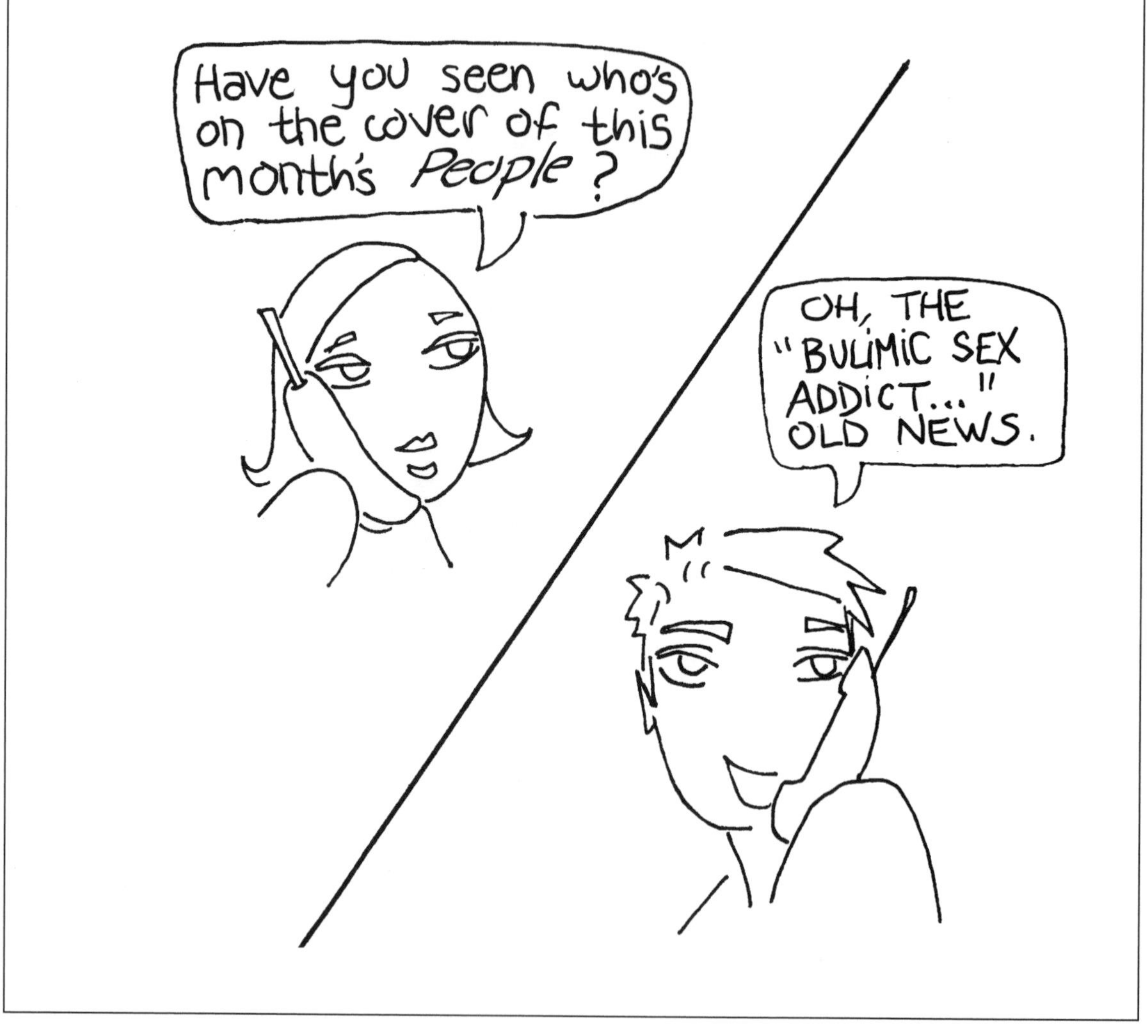

. . . gossip . . .

CELEBRITY GOSSIP

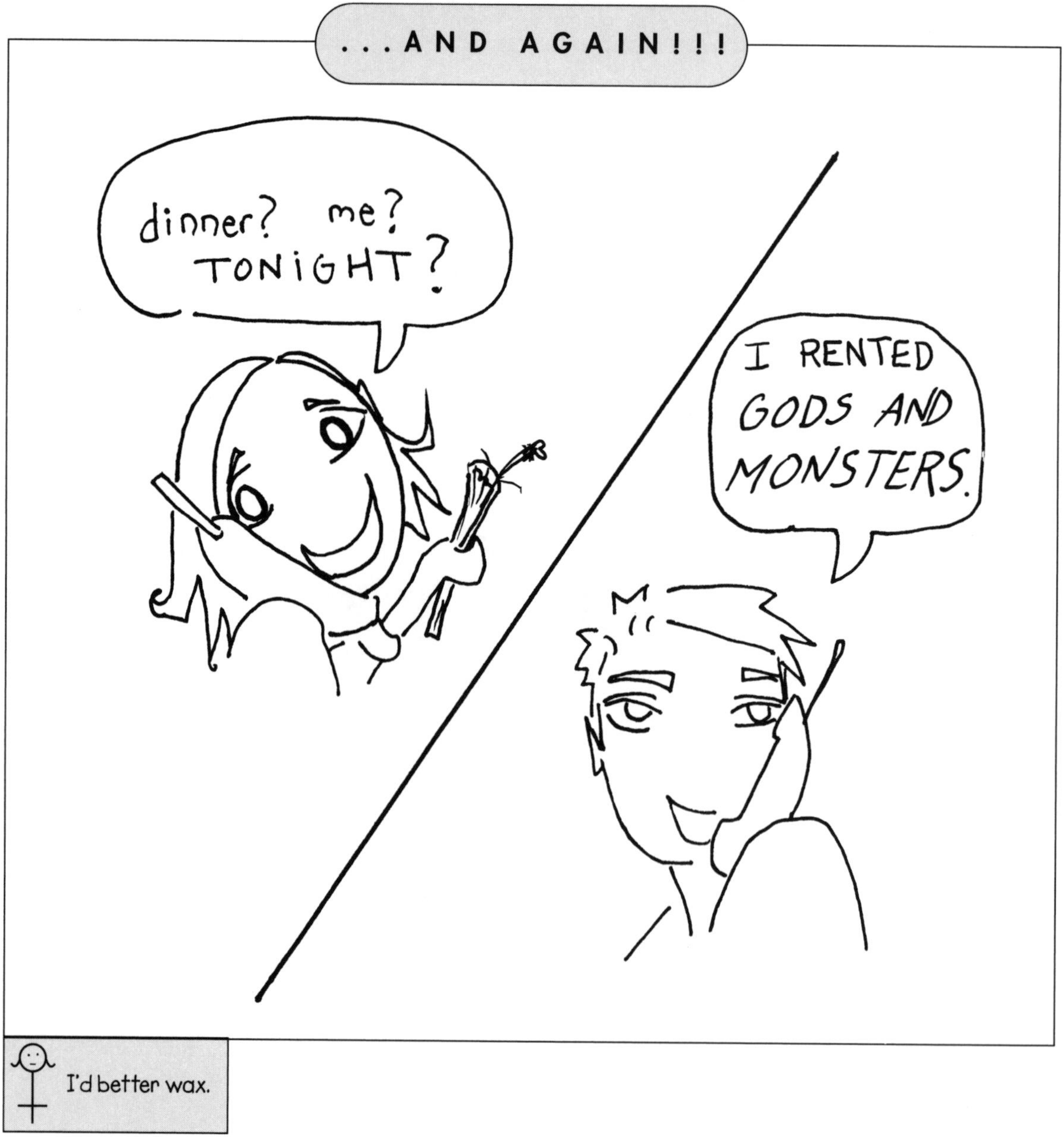
...AND AGAIN!!!
dinner? me? TONIGHT?
I RENTED GODS AND MONSTERS.
I'd better wax.

. . . last-minute invitation . . .

. . . he's making pasta . . .

. . . videos containing questionble subject matter . . .*

*Anything featuring Sir Ian McKellen, Rupert
Everett, Bruce Vilanch, or Tori Spelling.

HIS HOUSE (7 minutes later)

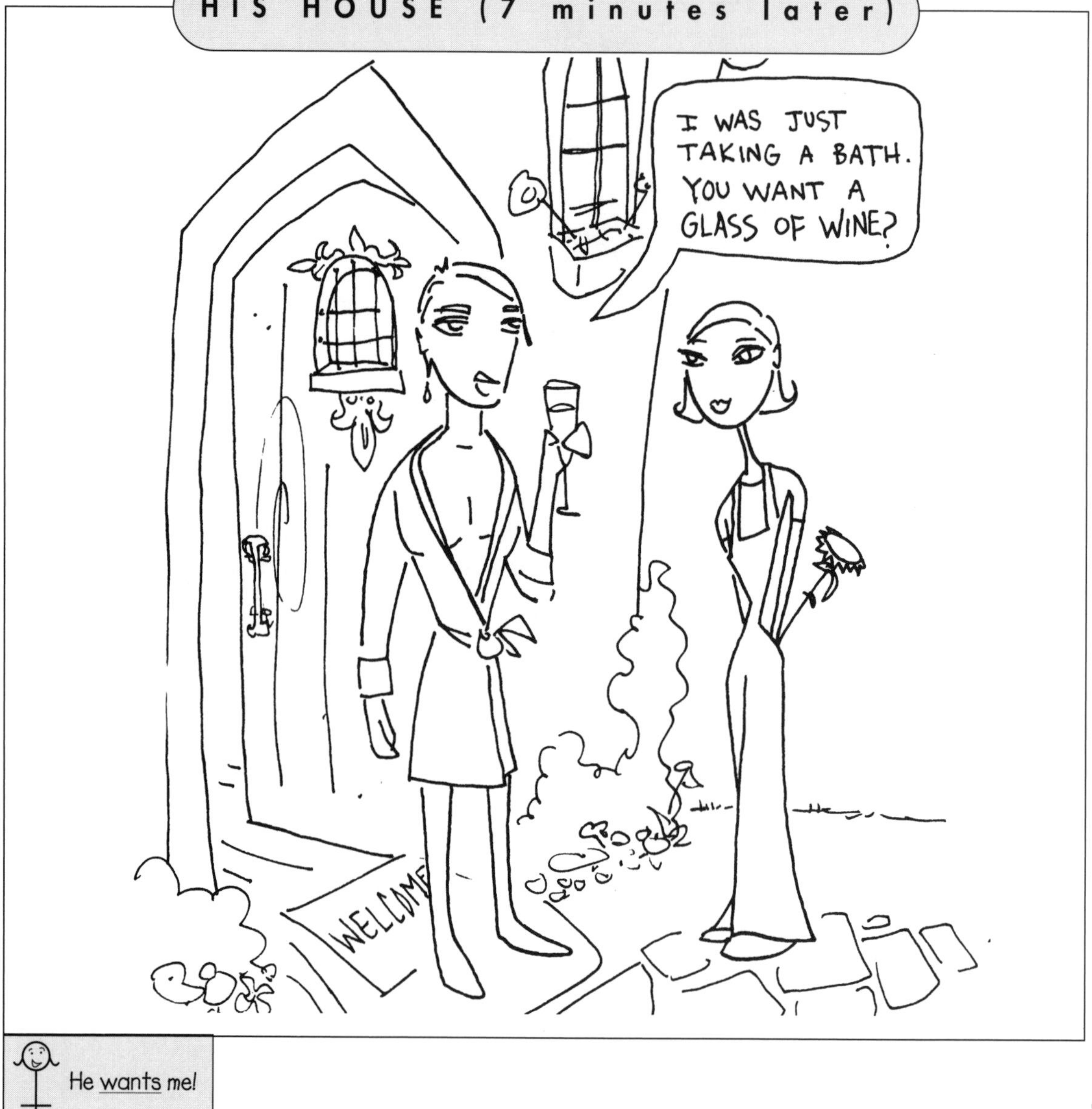
I WAS JUST TAKING A BATH. YOU WANT A GLASS OF WINE?
WELCOME

He wants me!

Hints

. . . drinks wine . . .*

. . . takes baths . . .

SUPERHINT

BATHROBE

*Chardonnay or champagne.

GETTING TO KNOW HIM

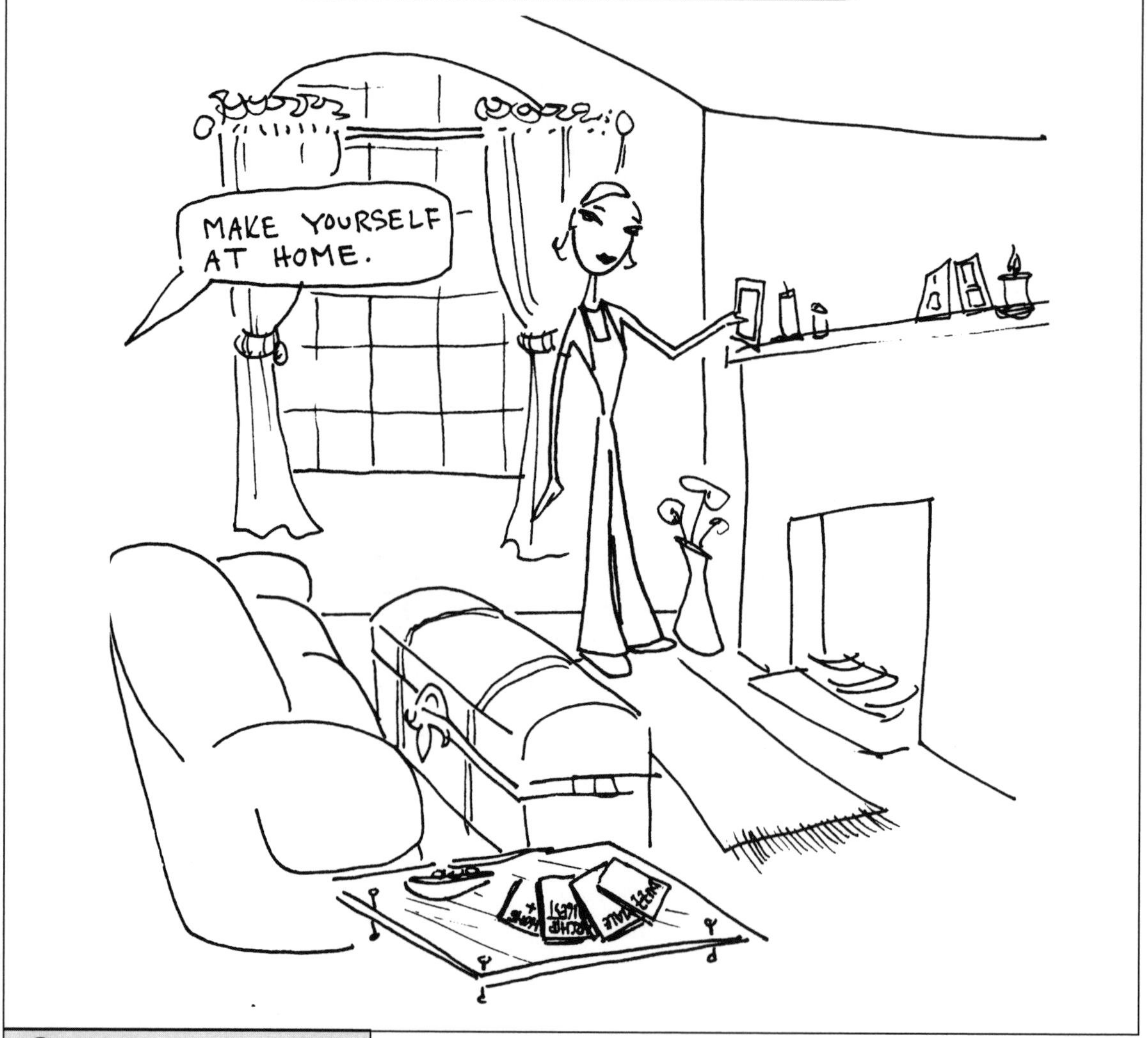
MAKE YOURSELF AT HOME.

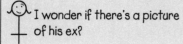

I wonder if there's a picture of his ex?

... he has great taste & he's neat ...

... drapes are billowy and tied back ...

... subscribes to ...
International Male, Architectural Digest, People, TV Guide, Wallpaper,
Exercise For Men Only, Detour, W, Vanity Fair, & Martha Stewart Living

... eats ...
stuffed grape leaves, cucumbers, yogurt, pine nuts, & feta

... drinks ...
Diet Coke

DRIED FLOWERS

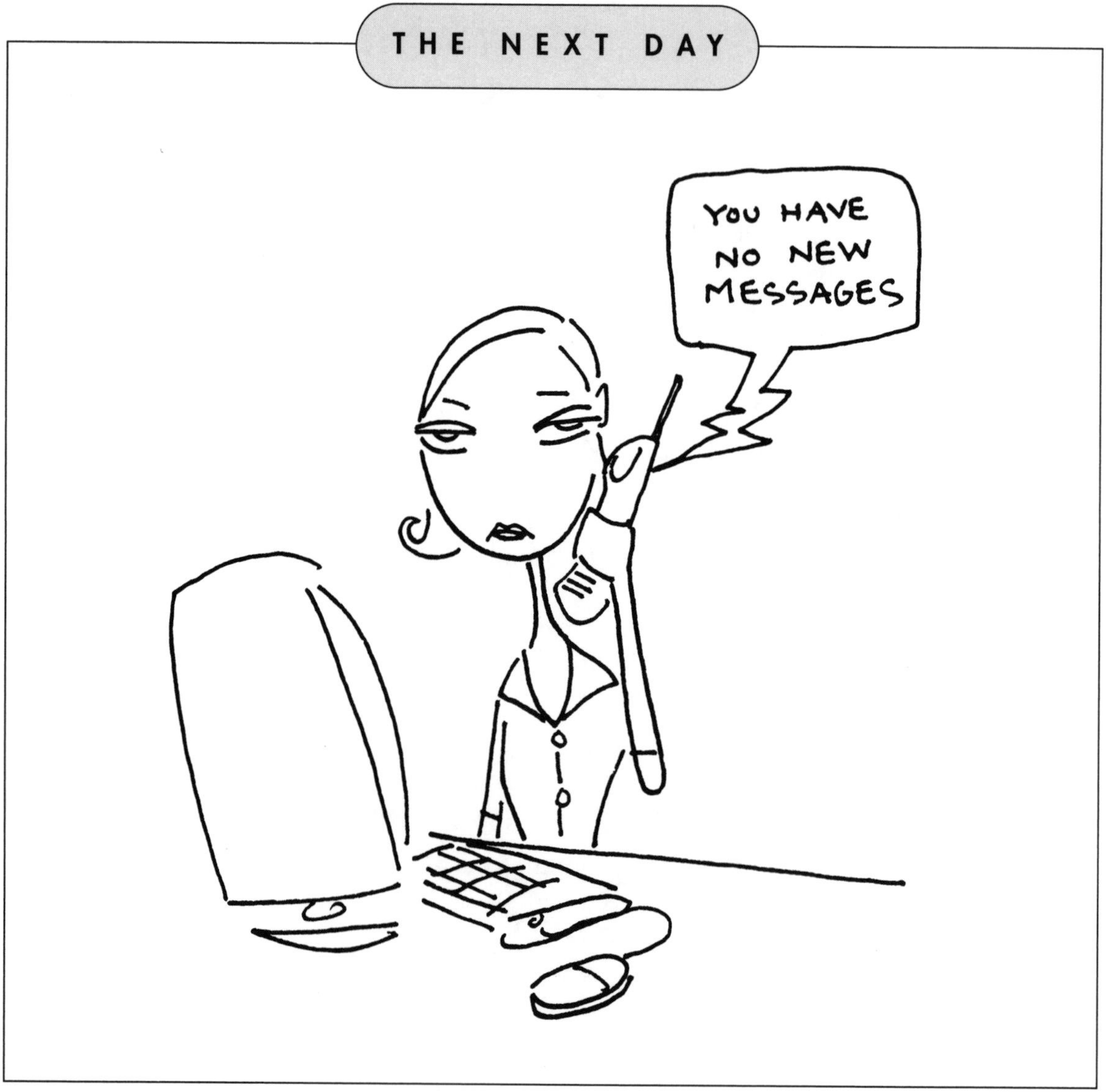
THE NEXT DAY
YOU HAVE NO NEW MESSAGES

THE DAY AFTER THAT

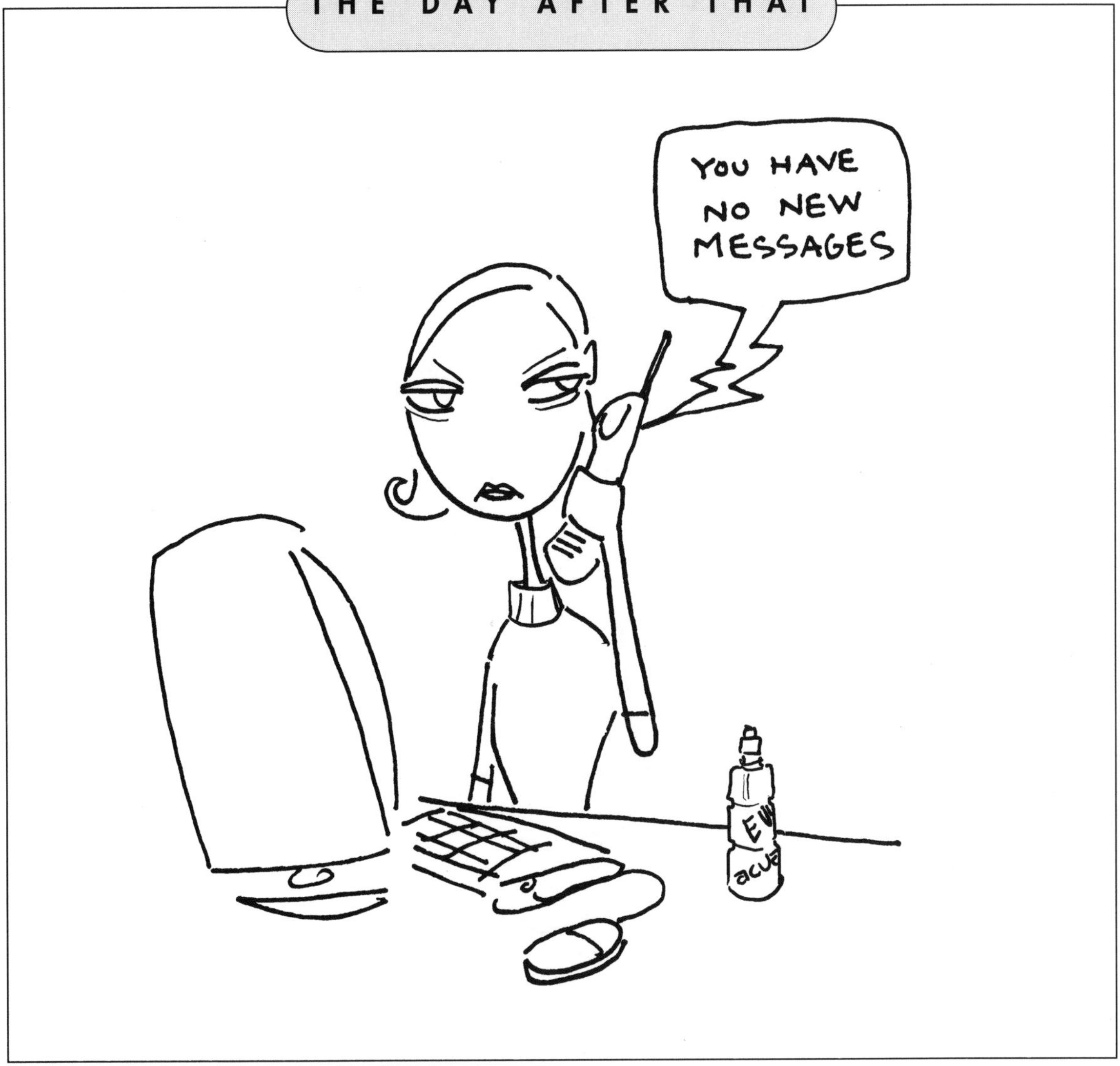
YOU HAVE NO NEW MESSAGES

THE DAY AFTER THAT

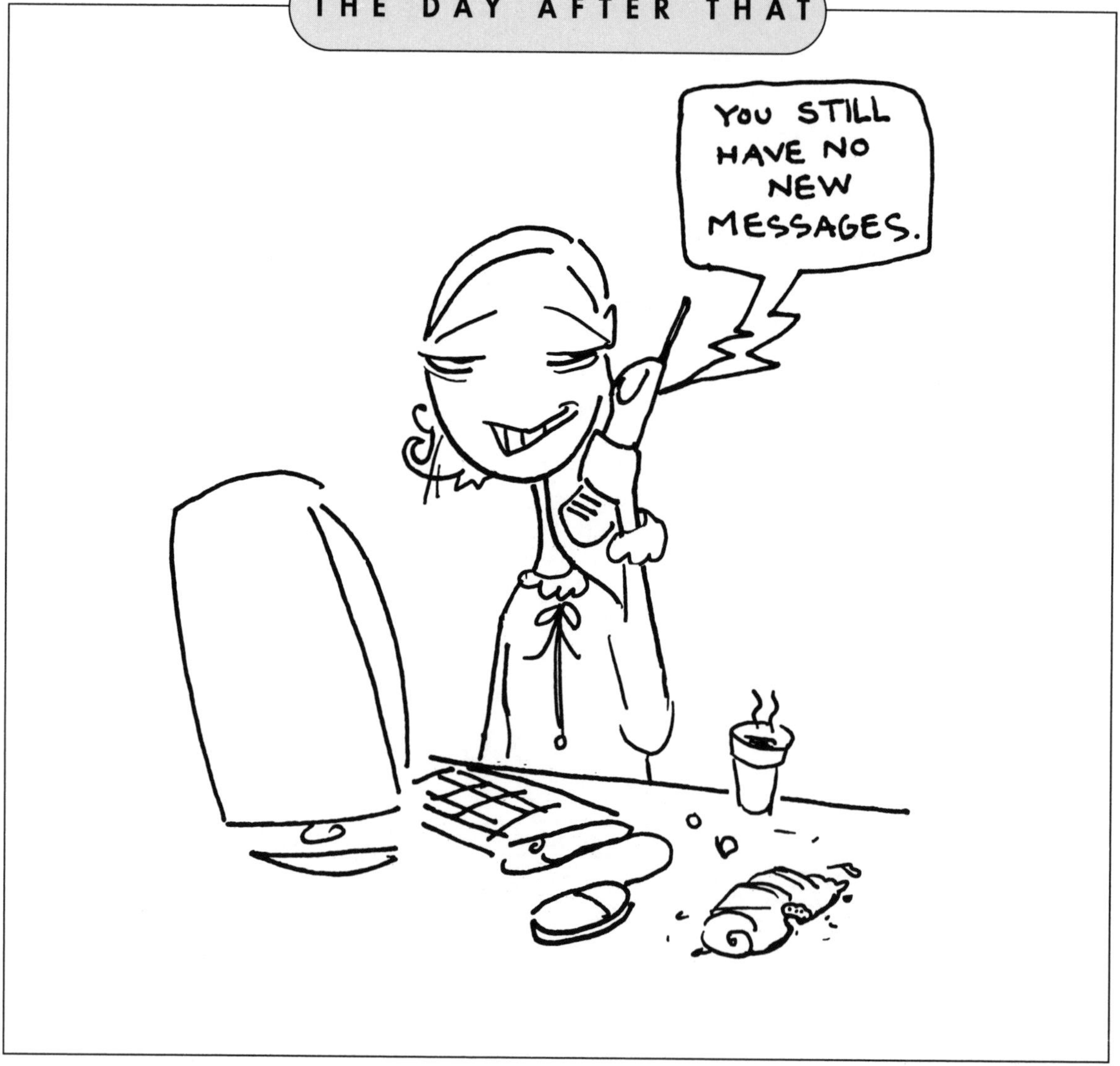

. . . erratic calling patterns . . .

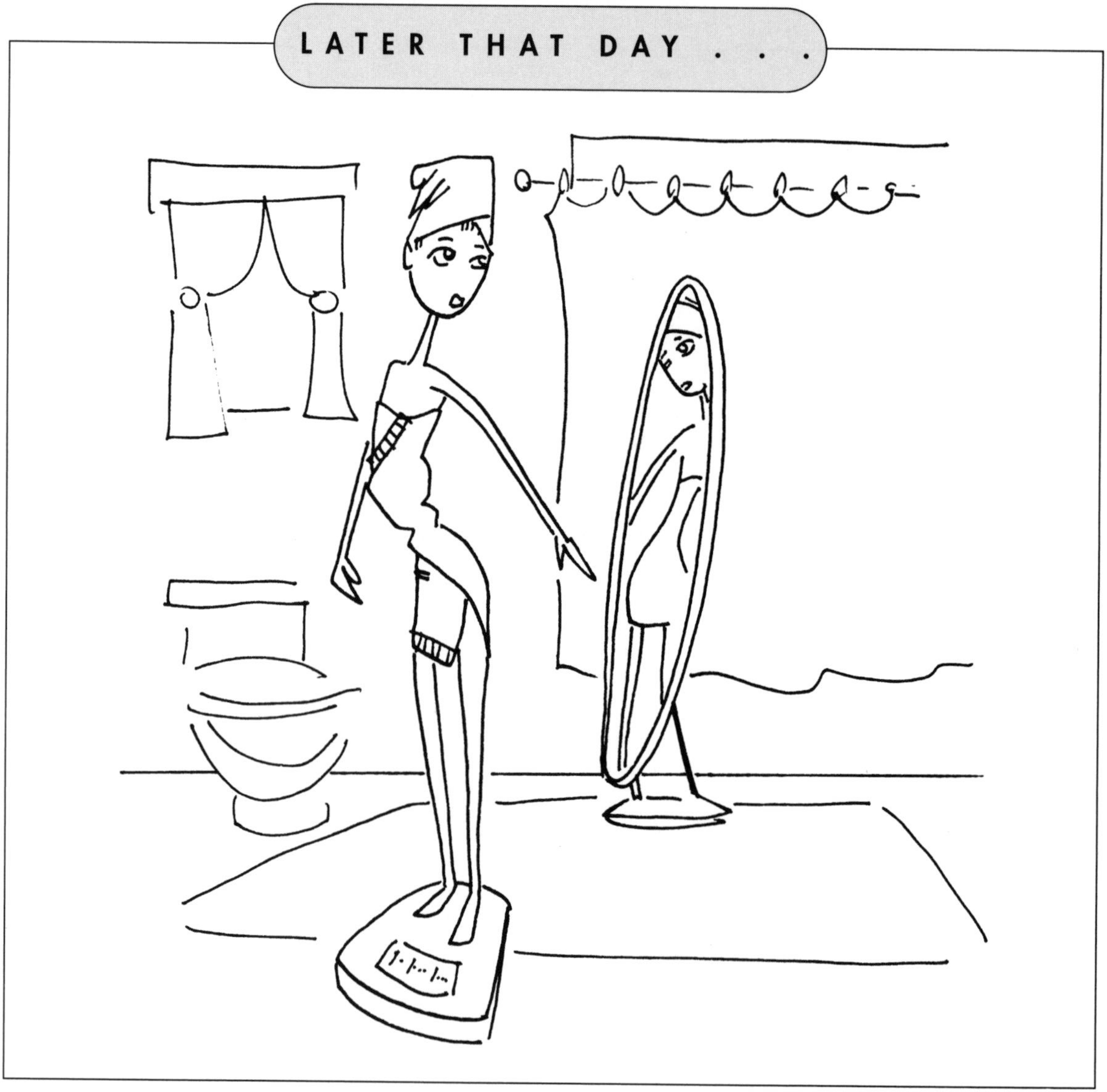
LATER THAT DAY . . .

It's my butt!

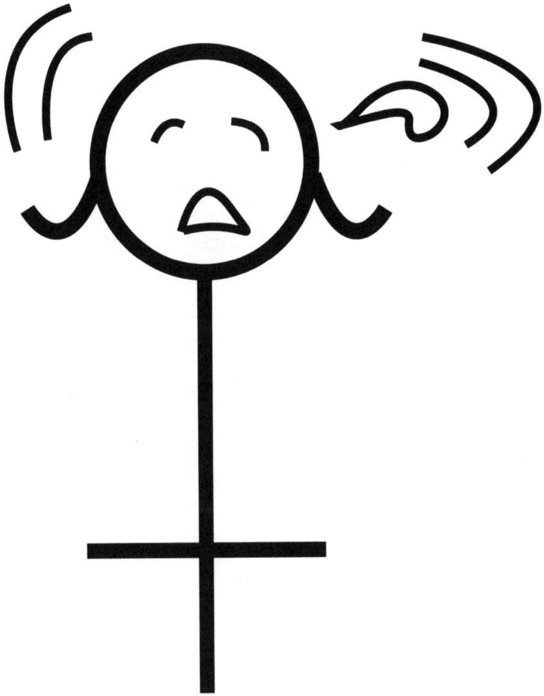

9:00 P.M. (Friday night)

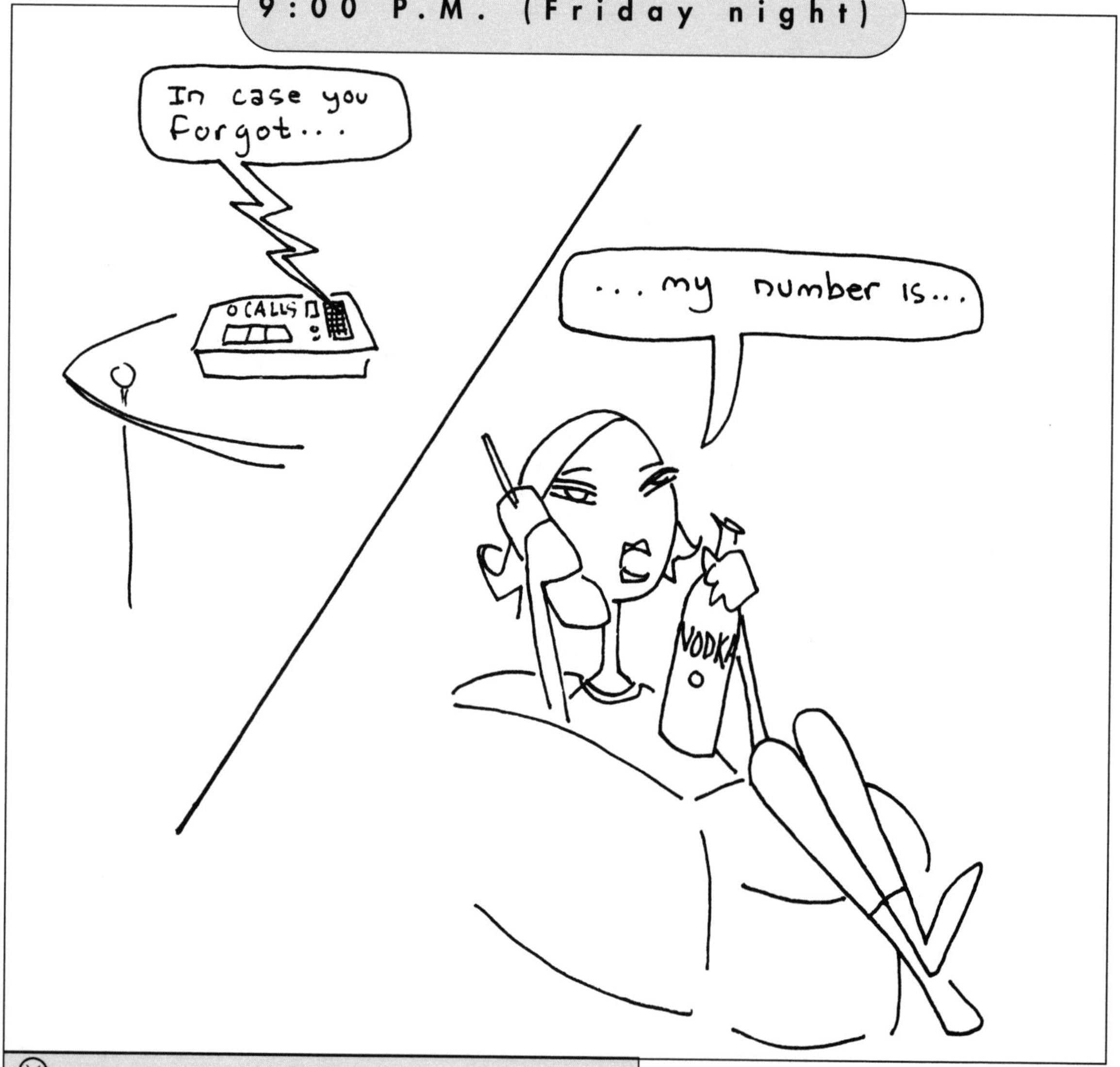
In case you forgot...
O CALLS
...my number is...
VODKA

I didn't like him anyway, thank God I didn't sleep with him!

. . . he didn't sleep with you either . . .

HE DIDN'T SLEEP WITH YOU EITHER

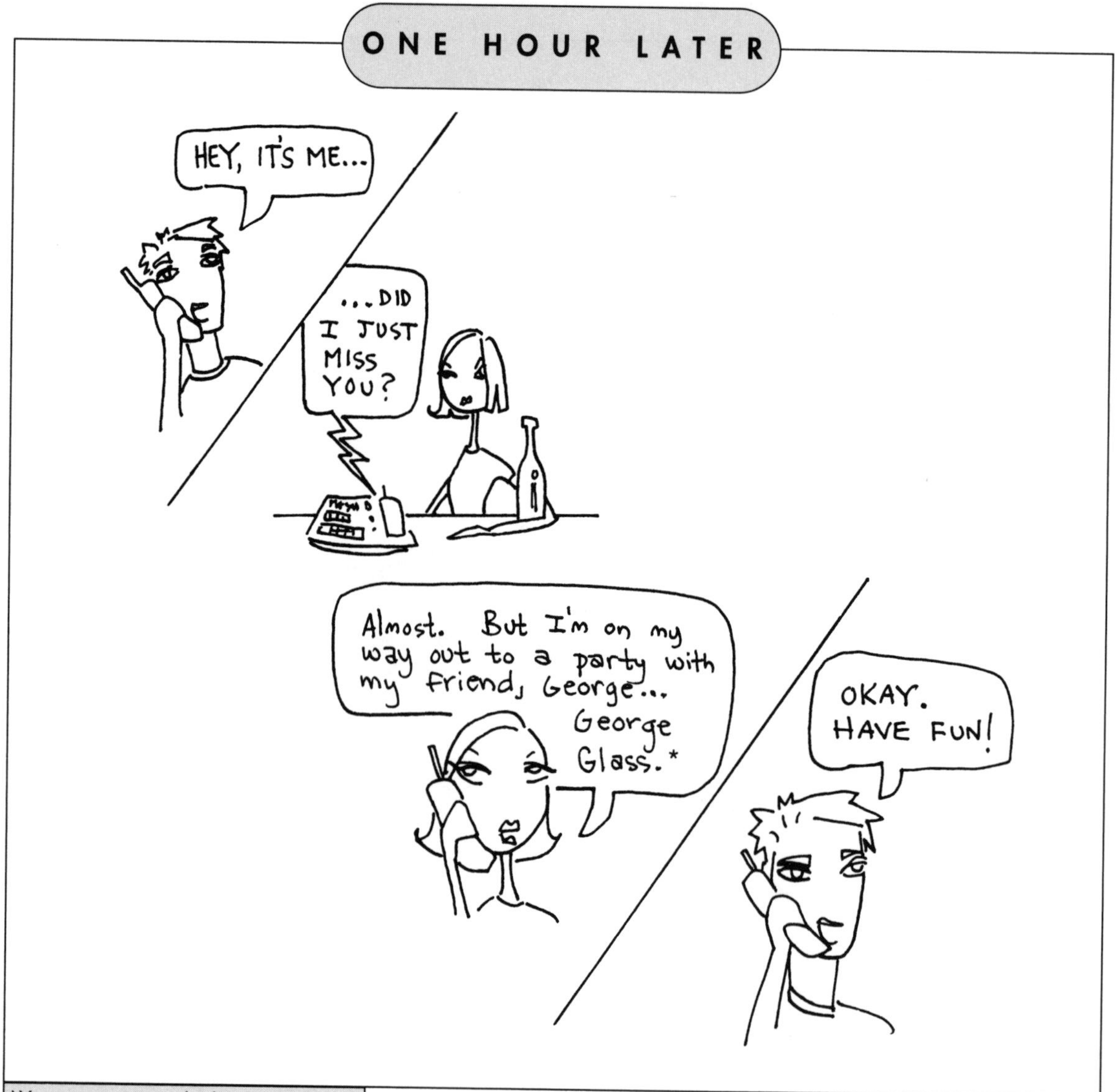
ONE HOUR LATER
HEY, IT'S ME...
...DID I JUST MISS YOU?
Almost. But I'm on my way out to a party with my friend, George... George Glass.*
OKAY. HAVE FUN!

*You attempt to make him jealous . . . (you lie).

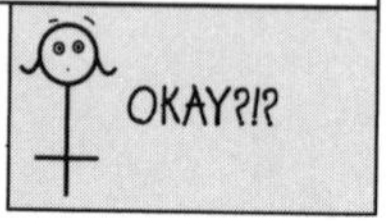
OKAY?!?

. . . he's not jealous . . .

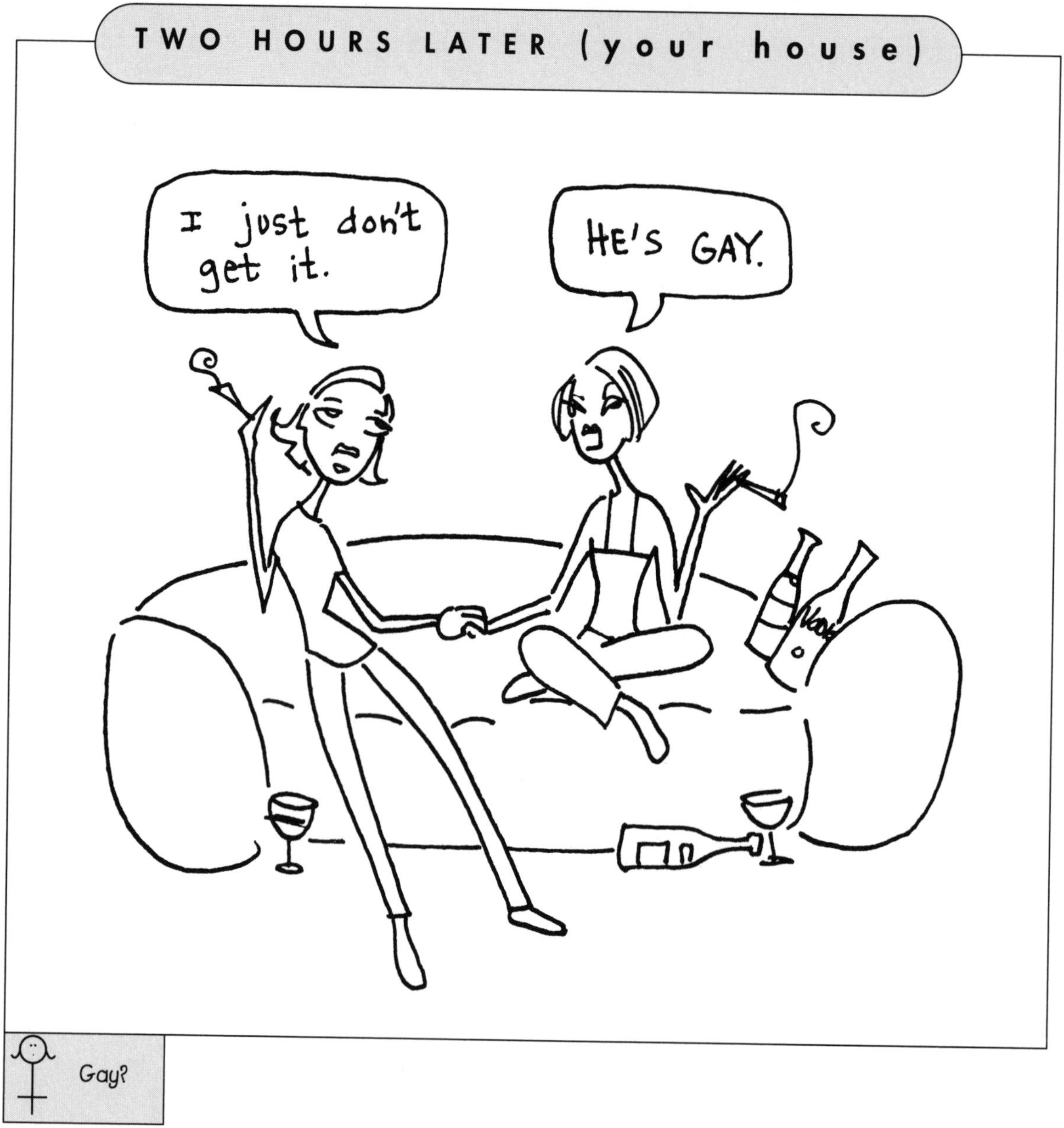
TWO HOURS LATER (your house)
I just don't get it.
HE'S GAY.
Gay?

Hints

ABBA	Disco	Masseuse	Tanning
Ab Fab	Disney	Minimalism	Techno
Actor/Waiter/Retail	Drama	Mirrors	Toys
Acupuncture	Fabric softener	Model hair	Track lighting
Aerobics	Facials	Musicals	Work boots
Altoids	Fat free (anything)	Nice butt	_____
Antiques	Female friends (single)	Oprah	_____
Aromatherapy	Figure skating	Palm Springs	_____
Art	Finicky	Panic attacks	_____
Astrology	Flavored vodka	Pedicures	_____
Backpacks	Flea markets	Pee shy	_____
Bed Bath & Beyond	Flight attendant	Photography	_____
Blow dryer	Gym (multimemberships)	Pilates	_____
Blow pops	Hairspray	Plants	_____
Body hair (minimal)	Health food	Pool parties	_____
Briefs	Helpful	Potpourri	_____
Camp	Highlights	Preferred Seating	_____
Cats	Hissy fits	Quasi-British accent	_____
Chamomile tea	IKEA	Quasi-southern accent	_____
Chelsea	Japanimation	Rubbernecking	_____
CK (anything)	Juice bars	Sensitive	_____
Clinique	Jeeps	Short shorts	_____
Colored contacts	Karaoke (taken seriously)	South Beach	_____
Corona (with lime)	Knickknacks	Spice rack	_____
Cosmetic surgery	Linen	Stuffed animals	_____
Crossed legs	Lip balm	Superheros	_____
Designer sheets	Lotion	Sweet 'n Low	_____
Dinnerware (matching)	Male friends (LOTS)	Tank tops	_____

INTERROGATION

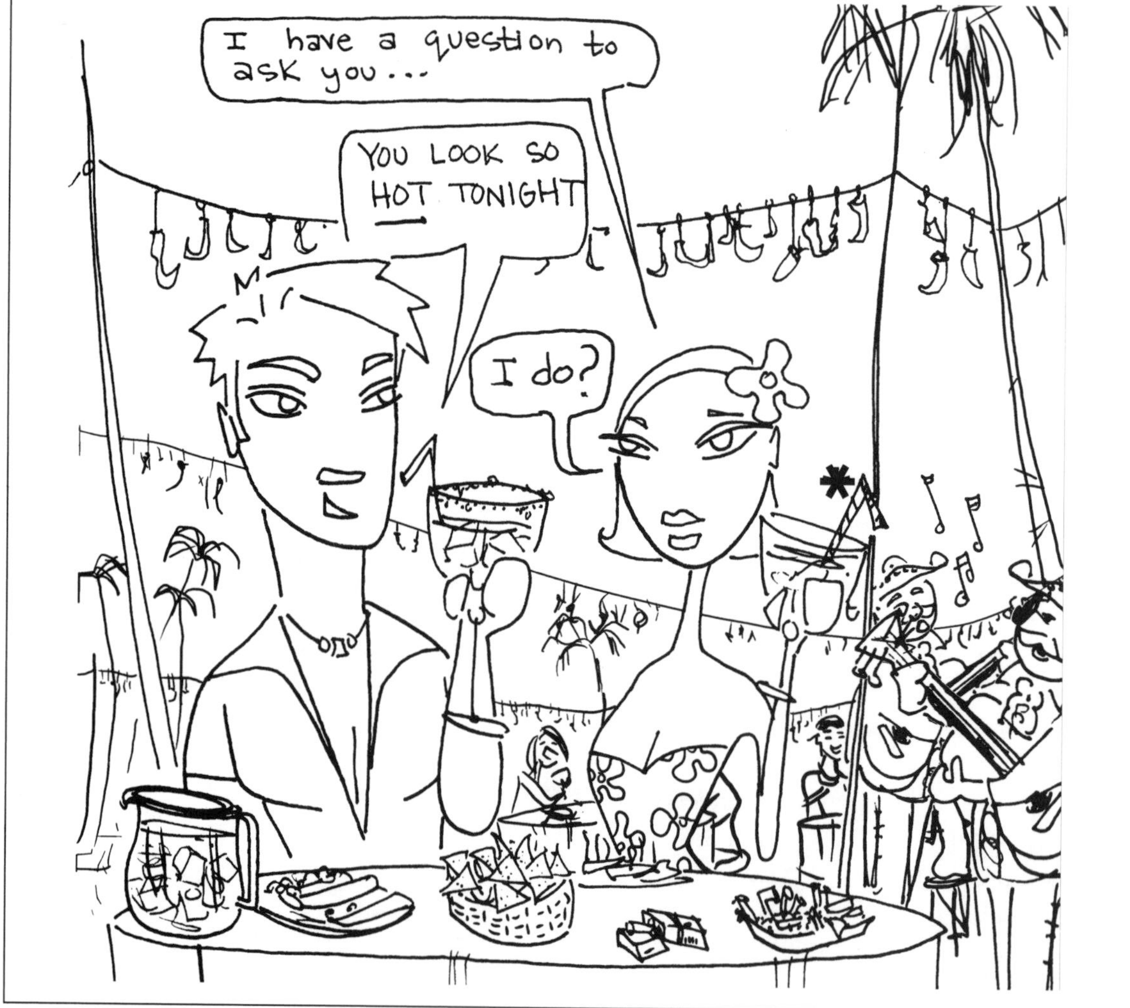

I have a question to ask you...
YOU LOOK SO HOT TONIGHT
I do?
*

*Margarita #7.

. . . flattery . . .

. . . Tex Mex . . .

STRAWBERRY MARGARITAS

SABOTAGE

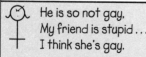

He is so not gay,
My friend is stupid . . .
I think she's gay.

. . . you're in denial . . .*

*Possibly, so is he.

DELIBERATION

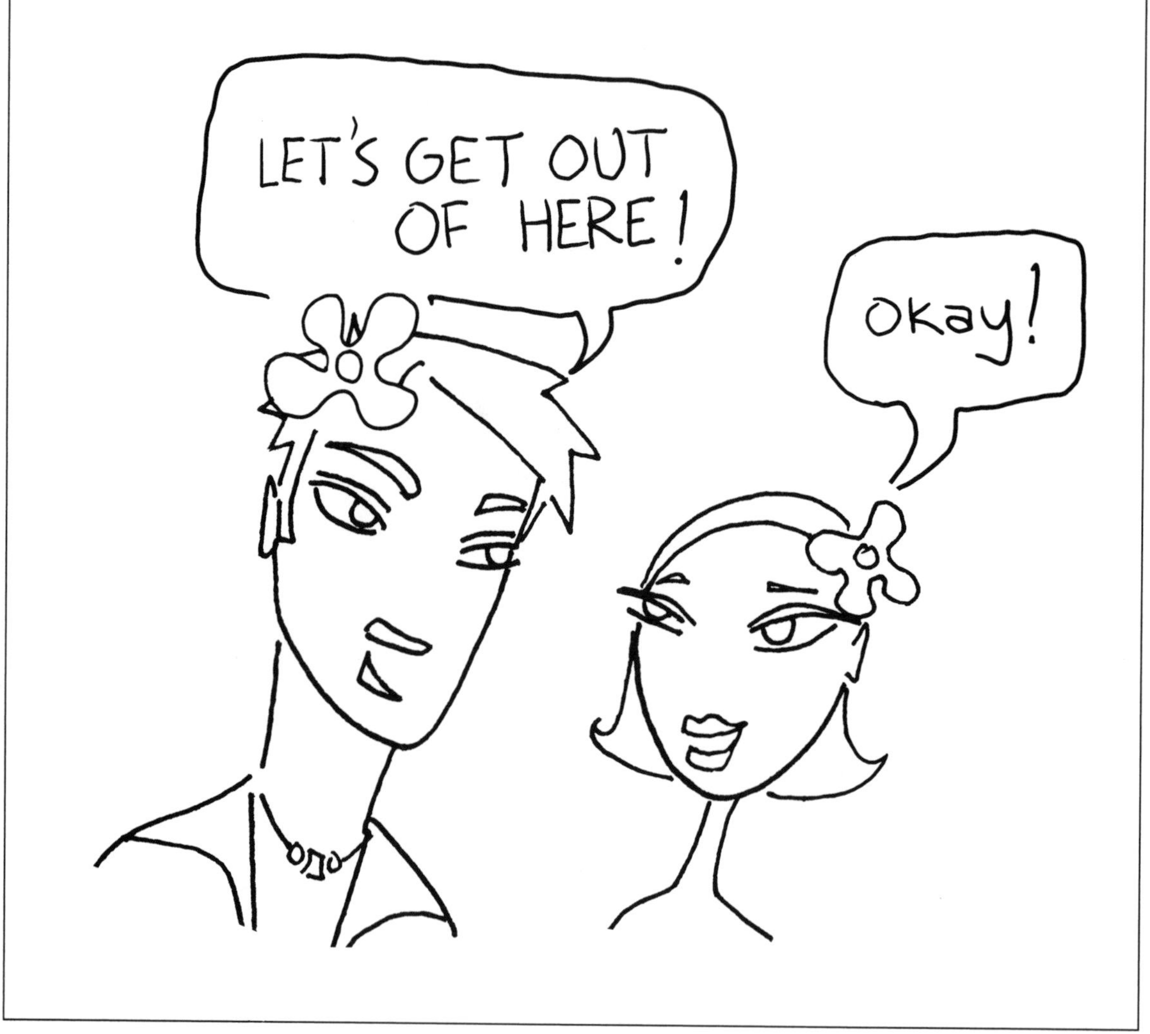

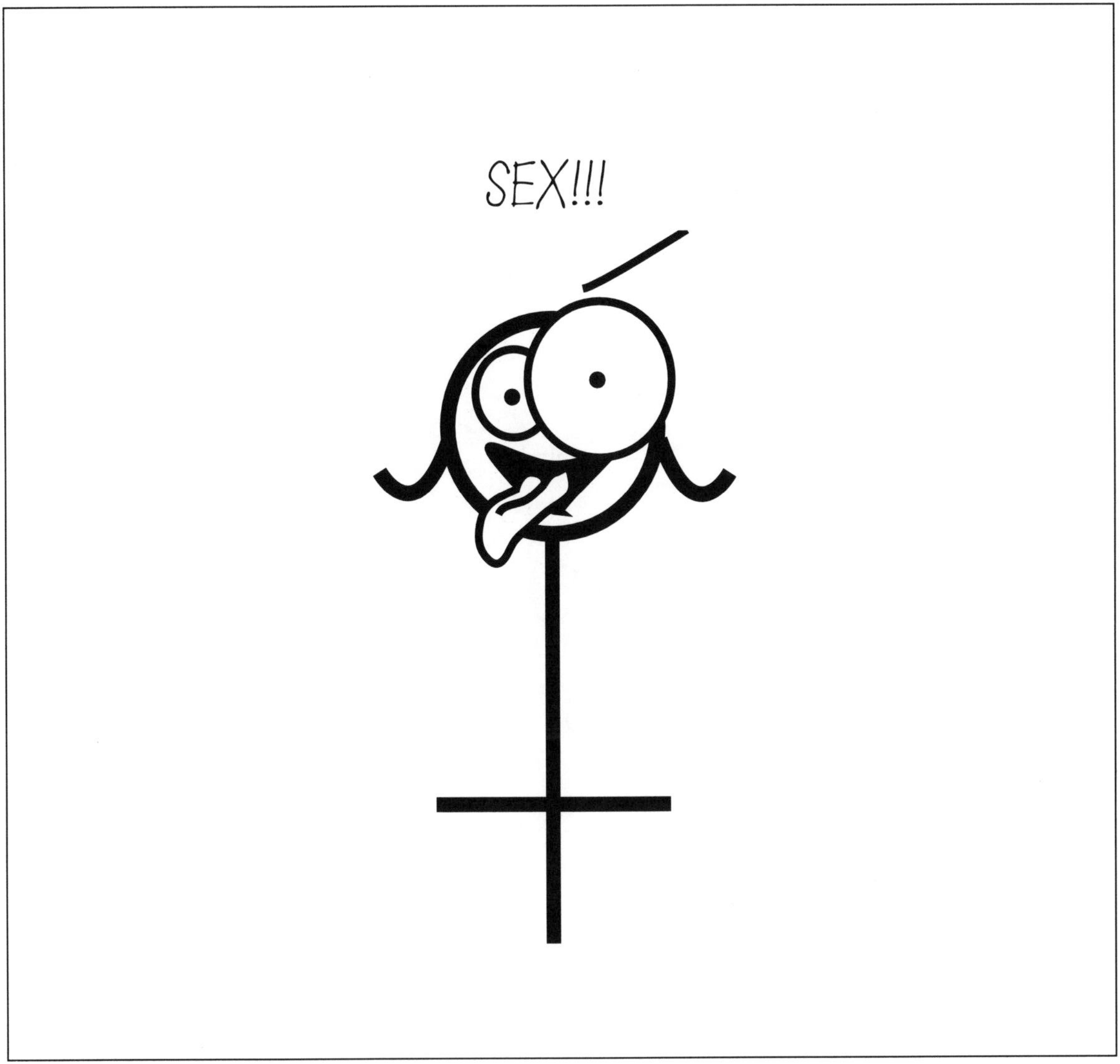
SEX!!!

SEX?

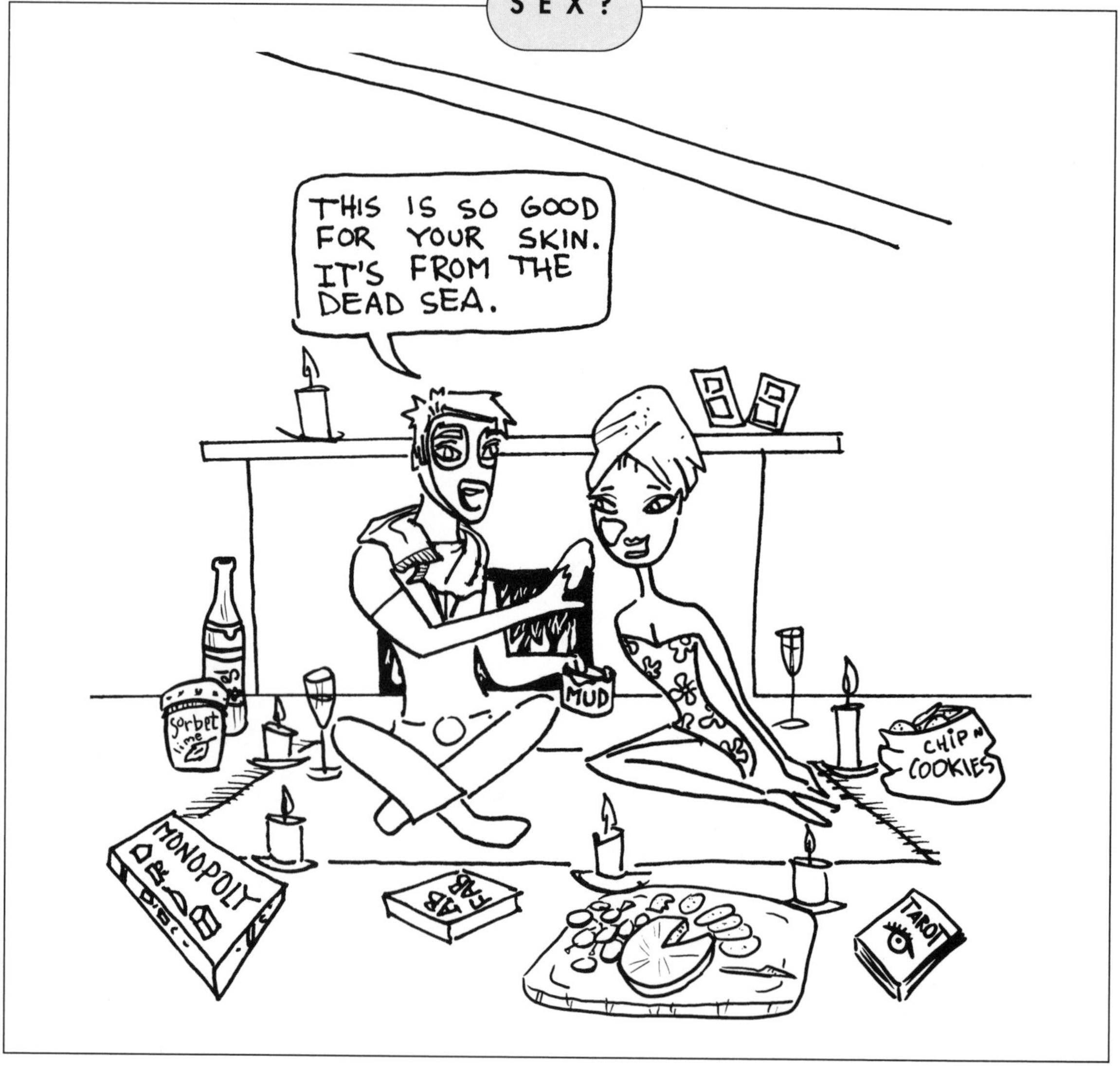
THIS IS SO GOOD FOR YOUR SKIN. IT'S FROM THE DEAD SEA.
MUD
sorbet
lime
CHIP N COOKIES
MONOPOLY
TAROT

VERDICT

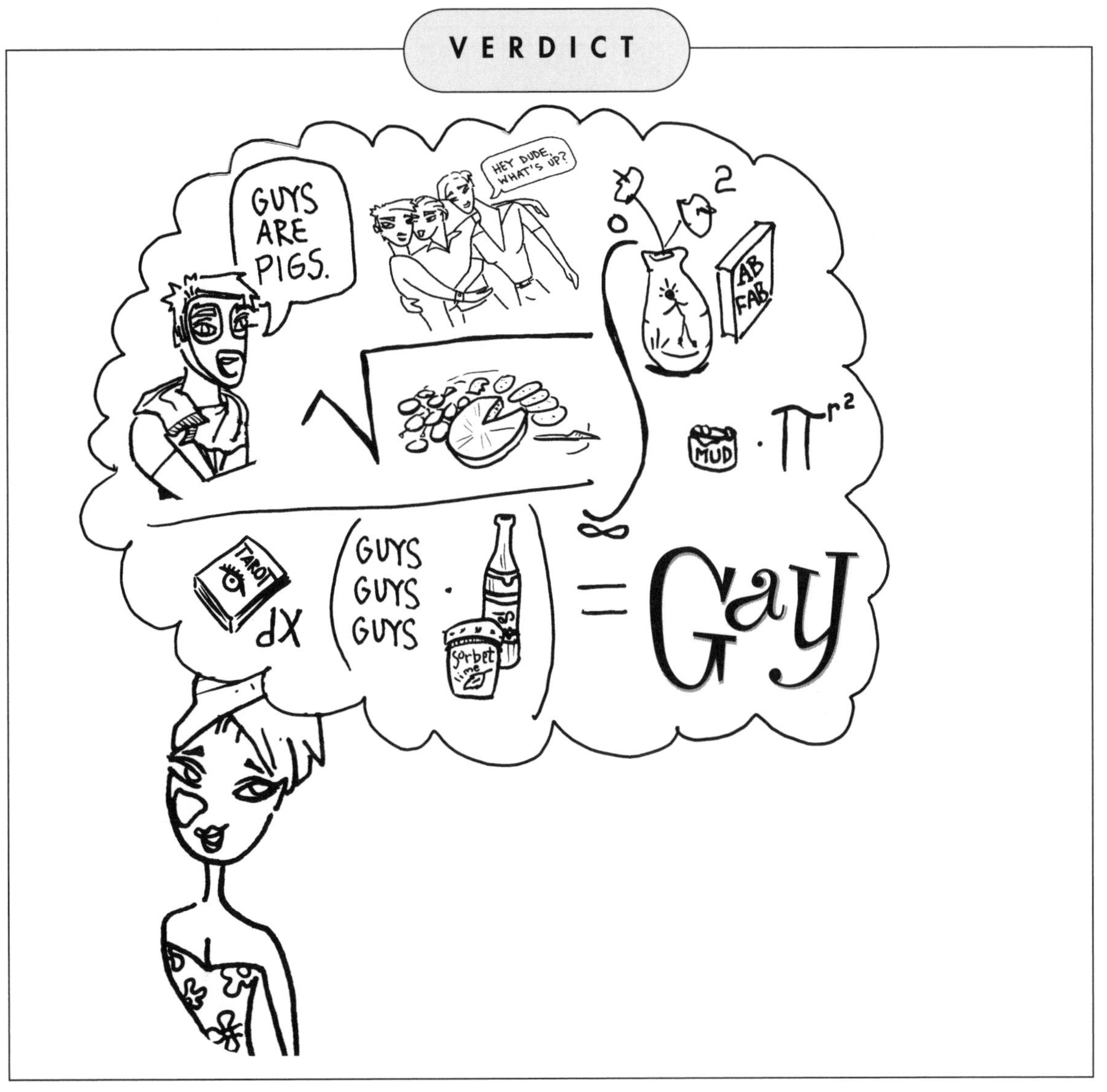
GUYS ARE PIGS.
HEY DUDE, WHAT'S UP?
AB FAB
MUD
TAROT
dX
GUYS
GUYS
GUYS
sorbet
lime
Gay

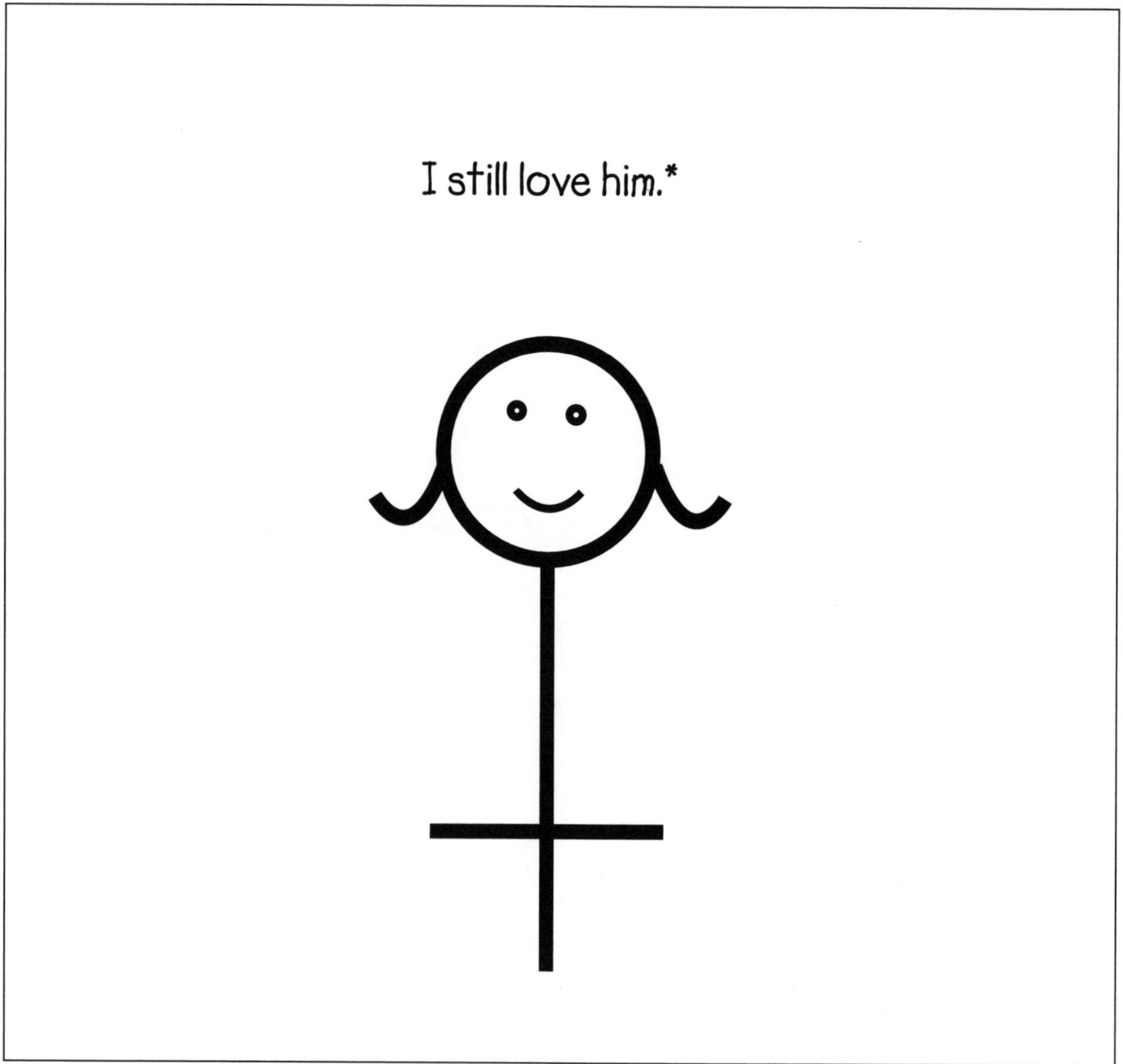
I still love him.*

*As a friend.

DISCLAIMER

The authors of this book recognize that the content is one MASSIVE generalization. There are bound to be exceptions. Neither author, in fact, owns a sconce. With that in mind, if you have any complaints, questions, or are single and too pretty, feel free to contact us.

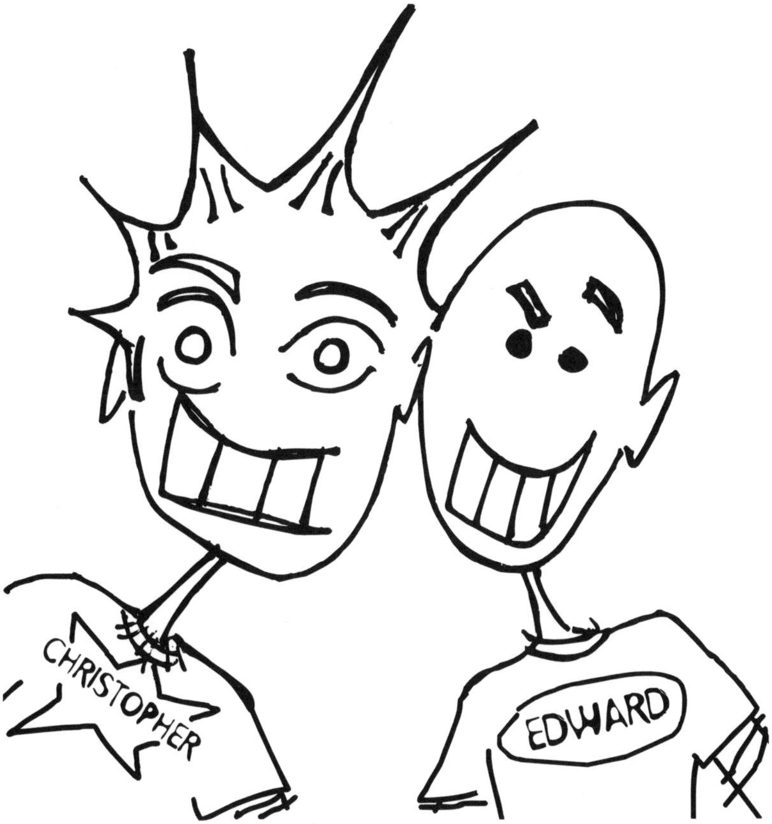
CHRISTOPHER
EDWARD